FR ANDREAS KONANOS

Strengthen
your Soul

Ἀκακία

Copyright © Fr Andreas Konanos 2013
Published in England by AKAKIA Publications, 2013

Fr Andreas Konanos

Strengthen your Soul

Translation from Greek:
Chapter 1: Heidi Alexiou
Chapter 2: Stella Savvidou
Chapter 3: Ioanna Alexaki
Chapter 4: Ioanna Alexaki
Chapter 5: Giorgos Migadakis
Chapter 6: Ioanna Alexaki
Chapter 7: Eleni Poulakou

ISBN: 978-1-909550-87-2

http://www.atheataperasmata.com/pandreas
atheata.perasmata@yahoo.gr

Copyright © Fr Andreas Konanos 2013
CopyrightHouse.co.uk ID: 144465

Cover Images:
Source: ShutterStock.com / Copyright: Ase / File No: 105338222

PUBLICATIONS
St Peters Vicarage, Wightman Road, London N8 0LY, UK

T. 0044 203 28 66 550
T. 0044 203 28 96 550
F. 0044 203 43 25 030
M. 0044 7411 40 6562

www.akakia.net
publications@akakia.net

2013, London, UK

TABLE OF CONTENTS

TWO WORDS OF INTRODUCTION

Nothing special. Just a few broadcasts that we made for the radio station "Church of Piraeus", 91,2 FM, now written in a somewhat tidy text, and translated into English for the first time for our English speaking brothers and sisters.

We spent several hours in each other's company, several times in the week. If I were to put a bookmark in this publication, do you know what I would use? I would use one of your tearful tissues. You told me many times that listening to my poor words you cried. We lived together moments of self-awareness, honesty, prayer and hope.

Many people have asked for this book to be published. Big deal! As if you do not know it all already... You know it all, trust me. You just want to hear it in a different way. You want the drug, but sugar coated in sweet syrup. You cannot stand injections, surgery, bitter flavours.

The truth is that it is you are who enrich me. You give me rough pieces of gold, silver and precious stones. And I take them, edit them and I give them back to you a bit more poetic, literary.

The raw material is yours. You just do not know it. You cannot imagine that your message, your phone call, your sigh and tear, your agony and questions, your sorrow and bitterness can become a radio show; that your sad soul can feed my inspiration so your feelings can become familiar to all those who feel the same way, through a broadcast. This is how I express it. I gather darkness and shadows of your own and my own life and put them in front of the Light of Christ. And just because it is what you say is true and you do not fake it, something true comes out of it. Hope comes from within panic; peace comes out of the mist, quietness and confidence through cries of despair.

Thank you for your trust, love and forgiveness that you give me. May God bless you always, may he broaden your mind allowing you to see far, clearly, humbly. Everything will be fine, all the difficulties and the crises will pass. The love and Christ are the only things that will stay forever and we will go along the way with those.

What is said verbally in the show can hardly be transferred to paper. The way, the tone of voice, the gaps, the colouring of the voice is difficult to retain in this transfer that we are attempting here, in writing. But it does not matter. It is a poor transfer of poor words. In the end poverty remains, to manifest that ultimately what enriches everything in life is love, with which we surround things. With love even the insignificant becomes important, even the invisible becomes visible.

Thank you very much to the organisation "Panagia Galaxa, thalassokratousa", which assumed responsibility for publishing the broadcasts in a book and to all those who helped and start this publishing effort. I thank those who wrote, corrected and edited this book.

The proceeds from this book and what will follow will be entirely for the completion of the church and the areas surrounding the hideaway that we are preparing at Galaxidi Phokidas, near Delphi and Arachova. I'm telling you so that you know. There, I hope, future broadcasts will contain more light, more views of the Heaven and the blue sky.

Since at Galaxidi, in Panagia Galaxa, the eye sees only light, sky, sea and mountains.

We thank all those friends of the broadcast "Unseen Crossings", from Greece, Cyprus and overseas who are already helping and those who will help complete the church, the cells and the utility rooms of Panagia Galaxa. Your deposit, however small or large goes directly to Panagia Galaxa.

The needs that deposits help cover are: the painting of hagiographies, pews, icons, shrines, floors, plumbing and electrical installations, library equipment, kitchen, rooms etc.
May God return your love and bless your life and your soul forever.

To make a deposit, please use the following banking details:

National Bank of Greece (Ethniki Trapeza): 040/296223-31
IBAN: GR8801100400000004029622331
SWIFT/BIC: ETHNGRAA

or

Bank of Cyprus: 0150-01-009645-00
IBAN: CY17002001500000000100964500
SWIFT/BIC: BCYPCY2N

If you want to wish something for me, let it be this: that I constantly make an unseen crossing from the appearances to being. This prayer of yours will perhaps hurt me, but it will be worth it. Thank you.

Father Andreas Konanos

STRENGTHEN YOUR SOUL

Translation by Heidi Alexiou

"Sometimes I listen to the 'Unseen Crossings'
broadcasts and I shed tears.
The point is to find the strength to apply
part of the nice words that we listen to
and to stand on our own feet..."
C.T. Chicago (e-mail)

My beloved brothers and sisters, friends of Piraeus Church in all parts of the earth, wherever you are listening to us from, I greet you. My brother and my sister, I wish you well, that you may always have peace and rest in your soul and never stop cultivating your personality. What I mean is that you should tend and take care of your soul and beg God to give you the gift which one day somebody told me he wished to receive for his own soul. "To progress" he confided in me. "I beg God to help me progress. To have my days pass by and always take steps ahead." This is exactly what people need, as a prayer of the Holy Liturgy declares, God to bestow "progress in life and faith and spiritual prudence on us." We should progress, mature and cultivate our soul. We should feel rested and contented, be quiet people with whole and integral personalities. We should reach the point that the Holy Bible mentions: "Attaining to the whole measure of the fullness of Christ. To the perfect man."

I know that this it is difficult not only to realise, but also to comprehend or really feel. However, I will give you an example in order to help you; I will tell you what it means not to be whole as a person, not to have a cultivated and constituted personality. How many times, let us say, aren't we happy, when we hear someone say some words of praise for us? How many times don't we really need a word of praise? We cannot stand being left alone, we cannot feel rested just being by ourselves and we constantly need a confirmation from others. Our wish for our value to be recognised is a permanent insecurity that characterizes us as human beings. I feel valued if you smile at me. I feel valued if you speak to me. I feel valued if you accept me in your company. If you don't address me, it means I have no value. This is exactly the point that Jesus Christ wants us to overcome, and lead ourselves to the wholeness of an integral personality.

I do not know if you have ever thought of that as an objective of life. I mean, to enjoy a moment of peace and quiet with yourself, so that you can stay at home, walk in the streets of the city, look, for example, at the displays in shop windows, go into a bookshop, and generally go somewhere all by yourself without feeling lonely. To find yourself somewhere where there are no people around, but be happy and feel that you have company, the company of yourself. But this sentiment has to be genuine and based on the wholeness of self, and not to be based on narcissism or the concept of "I am very important so I need no one," and of course, without selfishness or contemptuous feelings for the others. You should feel the completion deep inside you, and know that your value is not acquired through others but through yourself, because the seal of God, His image, His grace, and His breath are all inside the soul He gave you.

This is what gives you value and not what the others will say to you or about you. You should rid yourself from the insecurity you feel inside, and I mean that you should stop feeling worthless when the others criticise or insult you, or only feel your self-worth when they highly praise you.

No. You always deserve your self-worth. And you deserve it because you are a creature of God, His creation. Because God loves you and the whole heaven watches over you, takes care of you and gives you importance. Even if no one calls you on the phone for a whole day, even if no one speaks to you, there is a tremendous power inside you. You have value and personality. You are a unique being and there is no one like you anywhere on earth. No one is like you, no one has your traits, your gifts and talents, but on the other hand, no one has your problems, your peculiarities and your character in general. You are who you are and you have your own value. Jesus loves you and gives you importance. He wants to strengthen you.

This is the key-phrase: To have a strong soul. To build your own personal relation with Christ and find the golden ratio of communication. However, you should build such a relationship with Him that will not isolate you from the company of your brothers, for example, the devout members of your parish, or prevent you from going to a meeting. You must not isolate yourself, but you must not try to consort with others in order to acquire value, because value cannot be acquired in such a way. You have value. Even if you are confined to bed or to a wheelchair, completely unable to move, your value is there, even if no one pays attention to you.

Of course, this is easy to say and easier to hear being said. But the greatness is when this realisation pours out from inside you and you feel it. Of course, these are difficult things. However, I often find certain personalities in the

Gospels, and while reading the incidents that happened in their lives, how they dealt with them, how they moved, how they spoke to Christ and how they generally led their lives, I am convinced that they had such a strong and brave soul. "I'll go to find God and create a relationship with Him. Regardless of what the others will do. I don't care how people will see me or what they'll think of me. I have a brave soul. I have faith in myself that I can approach my God."

For example, I remember the bleeding woman who is mentioned in the excerpt from the Gospel. While Jesus was in a street of Capernaum, on His way to cure the twelve-year-old daughter of Jairus, "the ruler of the Synagogue," that woman came up in the crowd and touched the hem of His garment bravely, without first asking the Apostles to intervene. As soon as she touched the Lord's cloak, the fountain of her blood dried. Jesus suddenly felt that His power had gone out of Him, so He turned around in the crowd and asked who had touched Him. The Apostles were surprised and told Him: "Why do You ask? There are so many people near You. There are so many pressing in on You. What did You feel?" "Yes, indeed" He replied, "there are crowds all around me, but one person got something else from me, something that all of you have not managed to get. You are all close to me, but you do not attract upon you what I have to give you. You have me so close to you, but you do not take what I have. All of you.

The touch of the Lord cured the bleeding woman and He praised her for her faith:
(daughter, thy faith hath made thee whole; go in peace, and be whole of thy plague). That woman had a really brave soul. She must have thought: "I will go to find my God directly. I will not use mediators, I will depend on no mortals, and neither will I create idols, because God is not

an idol. If, on my way to find God, I use humans as my idols, deify them and expect them to give more than they have to give, then I will have failed. I will go on my own." That woman must have had a really constituted soul. Her body may have been bleeding for twelve years, as the Gospel says, and she might have spent all her money on doctors without result, but I think that her soul was full of health and she was really brave. That is the reason why that particular woman took something from Christ, while the others were not successful. Because, I think, she had that bravery. She had a beautiful soul which was progressing, and while her body bent to touch the Lord's cloak that was dragging on the ground, she remained standing tall.

This happens to all of us quite frequently, because we want someone else to intervene in order to help us get what we want, and quite often, we even depend on what they will say. We have become accustomed to having someone to act as a mediator. However, when you ask a Saint to become the "mediator" you have to be careful and fully comprehend and realise the way you will do it. You do not deify the saint, nor create a new idol out of him; you do not worship him, or put him above God. You just ask him to show you the way to Christ so that your soul becomes strengthened after that.

You should be careful who you admire and to what extent you admire them, because this kind of respect can be easily turned into a form of idolisation in the end, which will eventually distress, disappoint and hurt you. Because people hurt each other. Sometimes you think, "This is a terrific person!" "And the other one is also terrific!" You admire orators, simple people, or priests. Of course, you may question yourself: "Is it bad to admire someone?" No, it's not bad to get inspiration, to derive strength and courage but you must know the limits. I point my finger at the forest of Paradise, at God Himself, and you look at my finger and get impressed. You get impressed with the mouth of someone who is eloquent but he speaks about God. Your aim, though, is to go there, to God, because the mouth of the speaker is only clay, and if you don't go near Him, you will also turn into clay and then you will be disappointed, because you were not be able to progress spiritually.

People do not help or save us. You must accept it as a fact. Strengthen your soul and develop a personal relationship with God. Allow people to give you what they have to give, do not ask for more, and love everyone. But you should love them in the right way. Be compassionate and keep in touch with them, do not isolate yourself, and always have in mind that this is the only thing you can take from them and nothing more, because your God is there and He is the One you must constantly seek, not idols and replacements.

The Gospel mentions that when the Lord asked who had touched him, the bleeding woman came out of the crowd "trembling" and told him the whole truth saying: "it was me who touched you and that is why you felt your power going out of you." However, at the time a miracle is taking place everybody gets impressed, but then something comes up and man's faith in God is shaken. I think that more or less, we all experience such vicissitudes of faith. The moment you feel the faith, the fullness, the soul dynamic, and the humble, inner self-containment which come as a result of the divine ones, something happens and your faith is shaken again and you start wondering: "What is going on? Another problem? Finally, dear God, will you save me or not? All things considered, do You exist or not? Do You really love me or not?"

The same thing happened in the Jairus case. The people who were near him told him: "Don't bother the Master, your little daughter is dead. There is nothing you can do. It's too late." But Christ immediately turned to him and said: "Be not afraid, only believe." So don't listen to what the others tell you, you must have faith. That is why we should not rely on people. The same people who had seen the bleeding woman being healed just a while before were the ones who tried to prevent Jairus from turning to Jesus for help. The same thing happens in our everyday life. Those who say today "this man is terrific" may be the ones who will later disappoint you and shake your faith. That is why you can touch people but don't get hooked on them because if they fall, you will fall, too.

"Be not afraid, only believe." Jairus hesitated. "No, Jairus. You look at me. Aren't you asking me to heal your child? Don't you trust me? Aren't you calling me?" "Yes, but there are so many people around." "Live without looking at the people. See the world with your eyes focused on me." And indeed, they went to Jairus' house, and the miracle of the resurrection of his twelve-year-old daughter took place, despite the despair that threatened to flood his soul, not that he wasn't justified, of course. Because Jairus was a man who had feelings, and who felt the pain deep inside his soul. It's not easy to know that your child is dead and manage to have optimistic thoughts just because Christ is there by your side, and expect that everything will change. In theory, you may be able to accept something like that, but in practice it's extremely difficult to make your soul bear these times of temptation.

The difficult times are the ones during which our faith will go through a dreadful furnace, and our love for the Lord will be tested through big adventures and tribulations. We often think that we are ready to go through an ordeal, and tell ourselves that we have a strong soul and that we are ready to face any difficulty. However, the moment we say so, we aren't actually facing a problem. The soul falters during an ordeal. Your knees bend while insecurity and panic come over you. You feel the earth move under your feet and you don't know who to ask or turn to for help. To God? "But what God?" you say, "He has disappointed me at this moment. He, who was my hope a while ago, now becomes my bitterness again. He becomes my trouble. I don't understand what He wants! To save me or to trouble me?" This way, and through these blows, your soul matures. It becomes rich. It becomes cultivated. It improves. It becomes holy. All these things that the Bible mentions and which happen when you accept to give in, with all of your trust, to Him who wants to make you a strong man.

The ordeal that Christ subjects you to is often a very difficult one. Just like an exercise the teacher gives a child. But if the teacher gives the student a very difficult exercise, that means that the teacher trusts the student and thinks that he is able to solve it. And even if the student is not ready yet, he will eventually become. The student mustn't always solve simple exercises and there comes a time when he has to learn how to deal with difficult problems. By doing so, the teacher doesn't want to belittle the student; he only wants to strengthen him. This is the secret we have to understand and when we do, we will surrender. This is a painful procedure but it brings a brilliant result. It may not be an immediate result, but after a while you will be able to realise it, and people around you will also realise it. They will see that you have a personality, and that you are now capable of helping. Your word will be firm and it will touch the soul of your fellowmen, because it will be the word of a cultivated man and a strong soul. Think, for example, someone saying:

"In my life, I have gone through diseases, persecution, and unfair slander. I have faced irony and suffered great injustices." And another one: "My house was broken into," "I went through a big adventure," "I have lost a close person"… After all these, such a person has acquired a strong soul, he doesn't become dependent on people easily because he has realised the relativity of human affairs. So he loves all the people and sympathises with them, and this attitude, as a way of life, has a spiritual quality.

Compassion. People who have suffered in life are the most compassionate. They sympathise with people around them because they have felt the pain, and they can understand how the others feel. But while they understand and love them, they do not become dependent on them. They do not care about the others' opinions as they have overcome such things. Because in the furnace of the ordeal where they found themselves, all other things were regarded as trivial and of minor importance.

One day someone who had suffered cancer and chemotherapy came to see me. Fortunately, he had managed to overcome his problem and he was well again. So he said to me as a complaint: "Now, I don't have much time to read spiritual books because I'm too busy." Then I answered to him: "What can you read now? You have devoured the entire published anthology. You have personally lived what is written in the collected works of Saint Chrysostom and what is written in the patristic texts about pain, patience, prayer and endurance. You have put in practice the Patristic Theology and the lives of the Saints because you accepted to cooperate with God. You accepted to cooperate with the lessons that God gave you in your life." Of course, I didn't tell him that he had become a Saint after all the difficulties he had gone through, because this way, anyone who went through pain would become a Saint. But this is not the case. Everybody goes through pain. But not everybody becomes a saint, because some of them react, feel indignation, and refuse to learn the lesson God gives them through hardships. And they insist on their own way, refusing to mature. But if someone cooperates, he cultivates his personality to the fullest.

Once I was told: "You must, when you think of yourself in the past, feel that you don't like much the way you were. You should feel that you continuously change, that everything old in you dies and that something new is always born." The meaning of these words is that you must become a different person every day. You should broaden your mind and your thoughts, and adopt a new perspective on life. Something old should die within you and something new should resurrect. In essence, as the years go by, and as one finds himself closer to God, he loves Him and prays, and as he struggles and tries for the best in his everyday life, he changes, he gains and he realises new, positive parts of himself. Through the pain that he feels at times, through maturity and through the effort that he makes, he realises the change that Christ brings to his life.

One more excerpt from the Gospel that I would like to refer to, is the passage after the Lord's Resurrection, when Christ asks Peter to follow Him (Follow thou me). Then Peter looks at John who was next to him and asks Jesus: "What shall this man do?" meaning, "I am coming, but what will happen to John?" Then Jesus said: "What is that to thee?" that is "Why do you care about him?" Here the Lord's saying may give you the impression of contempt, but it doesn't have anything to do with being mean or indifferent. What He really meant to say was that a person who exists in your life can willingly, or unwillingly, intervene in your relationship with God and have a negative influence. You ought to live your relationship with God paying absolutely no attention to what the others around you say or do. Each one of us carries inside him a personal treasure, his own beauty, which constitutes a special prayer. If you do not establish a personal contact with God, there will come a moment in your life when you will feel pain and you will have to go through trials and tribulations. You must feel God and ignore the others around you. You must conquer the Lord's saying "Follow thou me," because He loves you and wants to make you strong.

What really impresses me is the attitude of the ascetics on Mount Athos (The Holy Mountain), and how they live there on their own. They do not care about what the others will say, there is no one close to them – no one to praise them for their attitude, and no one to make any kind of remark. They have no interest in people's opinions, what they really care about is the opinion of God.

Can you see what God essentially wants to do? He wants us to become mature. But I don't want you to think that I have personally managed to put into practice all these things I am talking about. But I'm really jealous of the attitude of those people. Every time I read some passages from the Gospel, I think to myself, full of admiration: "This relationship between people and God is so beautiful!" God wants to make them mature, and make them ascend higher and higher. "Don't stay there. Come on, rise! Become holier and a more beautiful soul. Bring to surface this part of your soul which is hidden deep inside you. Be a little bit more patient and manifest this veiled part of yourself."

How can this be done? In all the aforementioned ways, with all the ups and downs. One moment you feel that you have

Christ and the next you feel you are losing Him. He comes and goes. This is exactly what His disciples felt after the Resurrection, when, desperate and lost in their thoughts, they were walking towards Emmaus.

As the Gospel mentions, they had just started feeling their heart aflame for Him, He had shared the bread with them, but as soon as they had started understanding the Lord, He once more went away from them. Why? To make them stronger. He only left a sweet sensation in their soul, warmth, faith and power. To believe, to touch and to feel the invisible as present. To feel that they hold the One who goes away but leaves behind Him His fragrance, His sweetness, His zeal and the yearning for Him. Then, when they went back and said that they had seen the resurrected Lord, they, themselves, were bewildered about what had happened. However, they confirmed themselves whenever they recalled the flame they had felt in their soul.

Christ wants us to love Him, but without having the feeling of certainty that we hold Him. He does not want to give us certainty, but leaves us suspended where we can experience the most exciting flights, make the most beautiful patterns in the sky of His love, and in the sea of life where we are swimming in its waves. You may think that you don't know where you are going in this vast ocean. Then He tells you, "Let the wind carry you away." "But I have no compass. I feel I have nothing." "Just give in and something good will come out of it."

If you can understand all these things, you will be able to realise how present God is, though you may feel that He is absent. You should know that this is the moment when you don't feel and you don't see and when you believe that He is absent. This is probably the moment when He has just given you His bread and as you start realising it, He disappears. In this way, He tells you that He wants you to have another kind of relationship with Him – a relationship beyond patterns, colours, visions, sights, touches and certainty. He wants you to feel in your heart that you hold Him there. Him who always comes and goes. Him who leaves His trace inside us, and Him whom we never know where He is. Him whom we cannot describe to others afterwards, but people can see something different reflected in our eyes, a glow, and they understand that the Lord passed through our soul and left something there. And this leaves room for fresh progress and new steps ahead.

And this will happen, as the Gospel says, in Eternity, in the Kingdom of God, where God will always be what we will relish, what we will enjoy, and what we will always ask for more of. We will ask for Him, however, not as something unknown, something we do not know about, but as something familiar, something we won't be able to satiate our soul with. Something we hold but always goes away. All these are interrelated, because they make you become a lot more powerful, to feel the absolute certainty and the absolute uncertainty at the same time. For all things in your life.

Maybe I could give you an example, to make you understand better what I want to say, because I tend to use rather confusing and contradictory concepts. When you speak to your child, giving him advice such as what to study, where to go, what he should do, but state at the same time that this is God's will, too, and that is the reason why he should follow your advice, the child feels a kind of security as to what steps to take because he feels that you know better. But your relationship with God is completely different. God constantly tells you one thing in your life. "I am the God of surprises. I am the God who wants to make you mature and make you realise that whenever you feel security, I am not always involved in it. I am also in insecurity and in surprise. I am in what you feel you lose, but in fact you don't.

To make it simpler – suppose that one day as your child leaves home instead of ordering him to be back at a certain time, you say: "All right, my child, you can come back when you think it's right if you cannot understand that you must be back at half past twelve. I'll pray to God to keep you safe, and you can come back any time God helps you understand is right." And while you think that in this way you let your child go completely free and maybe unprotected, you should know that you are closer to his heart just because you tell him " Come back any time God helps you understand is right," because this way your personal ethics and behaviour become more divine. On the other hand, in case you have a different opinion and you think that you can control your child by locking him up in his room and forbidding him to go out, you'll see that your child actually goes away from you. In the first case, it only appears that you let your child go away uncontrolled, but the fact is that deep in his heart, your child will always feel close to you. The child says: "While my mother and father were talking to me I felt my heart burning. I won't come back at three in the morning. I'll be back earlier" or "I'll come back at three but I'll be careful. I'll behave myself and act as if both my parents were present. I won't do anything bad or ugly, I won't indulge in substance abuse or get drunk, and I definitely won't act like a tramp or be foul-mouthed."

I mentioned all these things to give you a better understanding of what the meaning of essential and not superficial security is. What security basically is, and what the everyday plans we make in our life mean. Christ says: "I have no plans. I did things without planning them, things that meant to surprise and things that didn't fit certain profiles. But nothing was done without care and love, or without having order in my life. To put it simply, there were no days when I said that today I accept to meet people but tomorrow I won't. Today I'm going to this house, today I'm visiting those who are decent, tomorrow the sinners..." Simplicity. Whatever God sends your way. Life cannot fit certain profiles and it cannot be programmed. However much you may want it, it is not possible. Neither God, nor His affairs, nor the way He governs our lives.

All those things I am talking about are things that I see happening in the everyday life of ordinary people, those who live next door, and the ones I could describe as modern "saints." These are things that include the fermentations and the interactions that take place in the relationships of people with each other and in their relationship with God. What do all these show us, then? Perhaps I could summarise it in just one sentence: "Get out of your comfort zone." Nothing is certain. Life is full of surprises and even God Himself is a surprise, so you must learn to adapt yourself to His own conditions if you want to acquire His morality. Again, if you don't want, do as you please, and who knows, when you are eighty, ninety, or older – as long as God lets you live - you may learn your lesson.

In fact, there are a lot of people who have finally learned their lesson, many parents, for example, who thought that everything could be put in a mould. They felt confident that they could rule their lives, their home or their family, but they finally saw that none of these was practically possible. They just couldn't rule. I have seen parents endlessly preaching to their children, in an authoritative way, how they should behave, but their children end up involved in gangs. Maybe this is God's way to say: "Take your lesson. Understand that you cannot be abrupt and you cannot be absolute. Open up. Relax. Become like dough and let yourself get fermented in everyday life. Understand my own ways. Things are not one-sided. Things do not always come as you want them to come, but the way God likes them to come. People who have a happy life are the ones who learn God's lessons and manage to adapt to his conditions."

I hope you have properly understood what I talked about today. But, beware, my brother. I don't want you to feel that because what I told you today deeply touched you, you need to talk to me and expect to get power from me, because power is something that you already have inside you. In other words, I don't want you to get hooked on me – or get hooked on anyone else whose words may have touched you. You should realise that you lack nothing. If you ever feel this need for someone, it means that you have low self-esteem and underestimate yourself. And this is not humility, it is weakness. It is not humility when you constantly complain that you cannot stand on your own two feet, because it's like insulting God. It's like telling Him that He has not given you gifts and talents, abilities, a brave soul and chances to fight.

Lean on the walking stick and cane of your own prayer and your own relationship with God. Yes, sometimes you may need the mediation of the Saints, the Virgin Mary, your Confessor and Spiritual Guide or the people who will stand by you. However, while mediation is one thing, dependency is quite another, and it forms a morbid relationship since everything depends on people. Is that how God wants us to be? Didn't Saint Peter, the Apostle, say that we should have boldness towards God and approach the "Throne of Grace?" With an open face, without covering it like Moses who put a veil in front of his face not to get blinded by God's radiance when he saw Him. Today, we go straight to God, we feel comfortable and that is the reason why we mature and make spiritual progress.

This is exactly the point I tried to touch on. I want to make you realise that we spiritually progress and strengthen ourselves in the struggle of life. Also, I would like you to make a prayer that all these things I'm talking about I may be able to put in practice for myself, too, and that God may give this gift to me, as a present. This means that we should not care about what the others do or do not do, in order to imitate them. We should have our point of view, be able to speak our mind freely regardless of whether the others agree or not, not to be servile and not to be affected by others. We should be able to disagree with someone, even if we have a really high opinion of him.

One day a child spoke to me about his Spiritual school. Once his Confessor had expressed an opinion on a particular topic – I think there's no point in mentioning the topic now – and while the student wanted to say something different, the Confessor didn't let him but imposed his own point of view just like an axiom. So the child hesitated and no longer expressed his beliefs and viewpoints. This is not a healthy relationship. Before God we can express our complaints, our disagreement, and our point of view. We are free to make our own choices, right or wrong, otherwise we will feel oppressed and both our body and soul will become sick. If our relationship with God's affairs is not the right one, instead of it leading to a healthy body and soul, "the healing of soul and body," it can make both of them sick. And because we are Spiritual Guides, because we are Confessor Priests, we are in a position to talk about such things, as we often hear about a large number of cases when people didn't learn their lesson, despite living close to God, when they failed to acquire their own personality and caused harm to themselves.

Consequently, it is logical to wonder about the use of the golden ratio in all these. That is, to be able to enjoy an independent personality but to be humble at the same time. Not to detach yourself from your brothers' community, but to be able to be isolated, as Father Ieronymos of Aegina used to say: "Be together with the others, but be alone."
This is the differentiation you should make, set boundaries and develop a discerning sense. Of course, don't expect to be discerning at the beginning of this path. This will be done as the years go by, as we become older and our hair becomes white, and as we become wiser and more prudent. Until that time it's natural to make mistakes. Until then we will say, just as Saint Peter said: "What shall these men do? What will happen to them?" and Christ will always reply "What is that to thee?" "Why do you care about them? You must strengthen your relationship with me, you must love me, you must try to look at me and care about me. Get your little soul ready to be handed over to me"… and then I think that God will take us with Him. When we are mature enough to be able to endure this long and lonely journey.

At that moment the soul shows its quality. What it gathered all these years and how strong it became. I think that it's then that God will take us. When we learn to stand alone before Him and with humble boldness we'll be able to tell Him "Our Father…" but also: "My Father…" and again "Our Father…" because we'll need to show Him the relationship we built with Him but without cutting ourselves off from the others and how we experience unity this way.

I hope it'll take years for this time to come, and I wish that we all live a long, long life, but at the same time I pray that these years won't just go by indifferently. I have the same hope for today, which shouldn't be left to just go by in front of you, but draw some important facts out of it: moments that God brought before you to make you mature. You will see. Certain things have happened since this morning but you still haven't understood the lesson, you may as well have missed it. A lesson in patience, for example.

Suppose that you missed the bus and you got angry. A lesson in humility. Maybe you didn't get this one either if, for example, someone talked to you badly at work and after that you swore at them deep inside, for the rest of the day. A lesson in love. You may have been successful in this one when you saw someone in the street, at the traffic lights, and even if you had given alms to someone else before you said to yourself: "I'll give him something, too. Never mind." These are the lessons I'm talking about. Lessons that I hope none of us will miss.

I hope the hour we spent here today was time not wasted. I also hope that you will forgive me because I take things out of my weak soul, things that may be wrong, spiteful or problematic... But I think that if you put them in order inside you, if you correct and clean them, you will be able to become stronger. Don't accept everything I say passively, think about them, and judge for yourself. For everything you hear, think of something better, something more appropriate. And when you understand what is really right, think of us who have made mistakes. And then, pray for us all, with your strengthened soul, pray for all our brothers in all reaches of the earth...

I WANT A SESAME BAR

Translation by Stella Savvidou

"...I was just listening to a repeat of the broadcast.
I wish I could make deeds out of what we hear from you.
I would really want to love those
that I do not love and that do not love me.
I would also like to truly love Christ".
A.G. London (e-mail)

The biggest miracle in life is learning how to love. It is putting into practice everything taught in the Bible, the Lord's teaching and the Saints' example; not just paying them mere lip service but making them your own, in real life. It means making them part of your everyday, incorporating them day by day and bit by bit into the very fabric of your life, in practice not in theory, dream or fantasy. This is the big miracle.

There are those who think that a miracle is an icon moving or shedding tears or blood. But "our" miracle, the life miracle we are talking about, is of a different nature, awesome, causing the heavens to rejoice. What really makes God rejoice is to see his people attune their lives with His. When His life becomes ours. This happens when what we say does not hold only in words and theory, but in practice. We can rejoice ourselves and we eventually become Christians in the real sense of the word as we let God come into our hearts.

I was struck sometime in the past when at the end of my talk someone asked me — "Is everything you have just said mere theories?" I was a little surprised at first with this question and replied that some words may appear as such, but in reality this is what the Church teaches us; this is what we are experiencing in our daily lives. It is everything we live for. Then he answered, "You said that what the Church teaches is what we experience. I know that the Church teaches this, it is just that I am not aware that we live by it. I must confess that I have never experienced this - that the words become practice. Can you give me an example so I can understand how to make the words in the bible part of our lives? Are we talking about real life experiences, specific deeds dealing with the present, or are you referring to another time and place? In this place, in the here and now, I have never seen this happening anywhere. I wish I had."

The first thing I would like to tell him is that there are many real-life, concrete examples of this happening. I wanted to ask him to travel with me to a place called Mount Athos where some people experience the teachings in their everyday life. But I didn't want him to think that this is only true for the minority, for the few people like Elder Paisios living there.

As our conversation developed it was reasonable that some of the audience would question whether the teachings could become part of our everyday lives or just confined to a minority, like the five persons I had mentioned. People wanted to see whether my teachings were true, or just theory. They wanted to be convinced that these things do happen.

All of a sudden I became reluctant to go on with the discussion as I was embarrassed. Some of you may think that I had to continue arguing with them, probably coming up with more convincing arguments. But this was not possible as I didn't have much to say. Unfortunately, I am of the same opinion, that we are not true Christians. Big words and few deeds. For example, one day as I was leaving the church a poor man came up to me asking for help. I apologized to him saying "I am sorry, I have no change with me, only notes". He then turned to me and said "I don't need change, I could do with the notes as well." A measly five euro note, for example, would have served a poor person like him well. Only minutes before I was preaching about love and solidarity!

But worse still I am condemned to repeat my actions when the opportunity for redemption comes again. Just imagine a new suppliant calling: "Congratulations father! You were so good in the talk you gave. I am calling to help you redeem yourself. Give me some money, I have great need." Will I repeat myself? I think I probably will.

I keep silent. I feel empty inside, I feel perplexed. Where are God's commandments in our everyday lives? The greatest miracle in life would be to experience God's commandments and not spend our lives in conflict, hatred, moaning, anything that hardens our heart and spend time with things that are not trivial in our lives. Jesus says: "Woe unto you, scribes and Pharisees, hypocrites! for ye pay tithe of mint and anise and cumin, and have omitted the weightier matters of the law, judgment, mercy, and faith: these ought ye to have done, and not to leave the other undone." [Matthew 23:23]

Surely many of you may ask which are the trivial things in life. Frankly, I don't know for sure. There is one thing, though, that I am sure about; we argue over things we shouldn't, even in the church community, things that don't have the correct order of priority in our lives, neglecting the things that are vital for human beings, things that feed the soul. For example, the Bible clearly states that anyone who has two tunics must give the one to people who are in need. Do we actually do that? I guess the answer is no. Society as a whole is not functioning based on this principle. There are some exceptions; but they are a minority, while our Lord addresses us all.

Jesus says, "If someone slaps you on one cheek, offer the other cheek also. If someone demands your coat, offer your shirt also." [Luke 6:29]. Who does this nowadays? No one. The excuse we usually find is that Jesus was speaking allegorically, symbolically. His words had a deeper meaning. But if you think about it, his words contained the substance. Of the two coats, give the one to people in need, if they slap you on one cheek, turn the other one, and never take revenge. Everyone, however, tries to find his own meaning out of these, perhaps because it is convenient, since the majority think that it is impossible to live according to Gods commandments. While we are clear in what we say, we usually do not experience it and we are totally inconsistent. It's awful.

Given what I have said so far, this is more of a self criticism. I was told once that I should argue with the people who judge God and explain to them what the truth is, especially to heretics. I am sure there are people who can do this, but I am not one of them. What would I say then to Christ? That, you know, I scream to people who didn't believe in him but on the other hand I refused to help the poor. Christ said "give everything." By the fact that I am a priest, according to the Lord I don't need money, a car, expensive clothes, or golden crosses. How I am going to apologize to Him? What am I going to tell Him?

If ever I dared dream of a dialogue between Jesus and myself it would go like this, to my shame: "Dear Lord, let me explain why I need all this. The Divine Liturgy represents the Kingdom of God, brilliant and magnificent as it is. So I have had brilliant and magnificent vestments made, expensive too, because they have to reflect you. Because during the Divine Liturgy I am not myself but I become your image. I wear these vestments to illustrate the eschatological perspective, the Light, Paradise itself." And the Good Lord will reply: "Well done my son. All this sounds good. But what about the poor man, the one you said you had no money to spare for. Strange that my own words did not spring to your mind then, that in his face you should see Me. That in the face of every poor man you should see me?" 'Truly I say to you, to the extent that you did it to one of these brothers of Mine, even the least of them, you did it to Me.' [Matthew 25:40] It appears you have fashioned a new gospel according to your reckoning."

I am repeating what I said and it concerns me first of all. I am not judging anyone. It is not my position to criticize and judge people. First of all I remind myself that the biggest miracle in life is to apply God's words and not just adhere to his words.

From time to time I reflect that giving talks and making broadcasts is the easy way out, because it is just a matter of charisma, a talent, a gift from God. Vanity of vanities I despair when thinking of the example of a booklover who came to me saying, "Father take this money and give it to people in need. Give these books to people who will benefit." Measuring myself up to such examples, I am all words and no deeds.

There are people who sacrifice themselves for the benefit of others with love, personal cost and personal commitment. They dedicate their time, money and travel long distances, even on public transport to serve their brethren. God perceives this as the acceptable and fragrant sacrifice, "To love your neighbor as yourself is more important than all burnt offerings and sacrifices." [Mark 12:33]. I am only full of words. We keep asking for a miracle in our lives. Is there a bigger miracle than this? Why do we need miracles? They come and go, you forget about all about them. You go to a sanctuary/church and you see a big queue waiting to honour a miraculous icon. Where do all these people go after this? What happens after the festivities finish? They will go home and return only if something miraculous or extravagant happens. What happens in their everyday lives, are they in need of a spiritual life, of a contact with the Lord? Honoring an icon was probably just a religious expression which lasts for a few minutes and then is lost. That is why Christ didn't insist on the external miracles. He wanted us to change from the inside, to give substance in our lives.

The Lord enabled Peter to walk on the waves. Is that a miracle? Does that impress? He didn't let Paul do the same thing. On the contrary he allowed him to sink in shipwrecks and tribulation. Some of us will be wondering why He did not favour Paul with the same experience. Yet Paul experienced great and deep miracles in his life in Christ. Even though Peter experienced such a spectacular exterior miracle, he was the first to refuse the Lord. Whilst Paul, who experienced an interior, very different miracle, got to know the Lord and never abandoned him. In Paul's life the miracle appeared in a different way, His boat sunk in the sea, he experienced difficulties fighting the waves, but he managed to come out alive and he thanked God for that. That's why when he talked to people his words touched their souls. Why was that? Because he experienced what he was saying, he talked with pain and love. The Lord was speaking through him. That is a miracle.

Nowadays we have difficulty distinguishing between miracles. For example, we see a bald person suddenly sprouting hair, we think this is a miracle or we see a person on their deathbed recovering and again we think this is a miracle. I cannot disagree that these are miracles, but a true miracle is putting to practice the Lord's teaching in our lives.

Many well known or recognizable personalities probably believe that by just talking about Jesus they fulfill their duty, since their celebrity status allows for a wide audience. Christ does not ask this of us. He just wants us to have a true relationship with Him. We may be well known, lauded by people, but He may "not know us," because our deeds do not speak louder than our words, if at all. We must practice what we preach, what we teach our children to do. Thus we end up at the point where I started this talk. Searching for a true Christian, an example, a prototype. Whereas we should have been able to say: "Look around. All of us God fearing people who love Christ are a living example, the living Good News (Gospel)."

Unfortunately what characterizes our times is exactly what the man said at the end of my last talk "Can't you see what's happening around you?" You meet a self-proclaimed Christian and you are disappointed. You think if Christians are like that it is better to keep company with anyone else rather than with these people. You turn on the TV and you listen to what happens with church people e.g. "A priest stole money from the church." It is impossible not to wonder what happens in the world. What happened to the Bible? Where is the Bible in action?

We think we are true Christians because we take Holy Communion, we pray etc, but this is not the deeper meaning of the Orthodox Church. It raises the question, "Do we experience this? Do we apply HIS words in our everyday lives?" That man asked me to show him some Christian friends, for example people who will not disappoint us, not people who don't make mistakes, but people whose happiness comes from their souls, where there is consistency between their words and deeds. Most of the people today are hypocrites, their beliefs are inconsistent with their everyday life. Our goal is not to fast just for the sake of fasting and showing off because this is considered right or even listening to the preaching and upon returning home forgetting everything we heard. We need to have quality in our souls, not just a fake profile to impress people around us. Since I am a priest I have to be genuine, I have to become an example to people around me and not seek their admiration or approval. I have to set an example according to what Christ taught me to do in my life. People justifiably wonder "Could you experience Christianity? In what planet? on earth? On earth we can't see it anywhere. Where is it?"

We realize that we have to repent. We cannot rely on the lives of spiritual fathers and saints to prove that there are people who have made the Gospel active and rich in deeds in their lives. This is the way we have to lead our lives. This is what Christ meant when he said, "My children, I will be with you only a little longer.... By this all men will know that you are my disciples, if you love one another." [John 13:35] It is so clear. His words are not symbolic. Where is this love after all? I am not judging you, I emphasize once again that it's myself that I am judging. I can see that I don't have true love inside me. I don't have forgiveness. I am not open to people. I cannot accept that others are more important or even more correct than I am. I find it difficult to praise the effort of the 'other,' another organization, another movement, another fraternity, another monastery.

The first thing we ask each other as Christians when we meet for the first time is "Who are you? Where do you belong?" We don't have true love among us. We are not connected by the love of Christ; we are really interested in trivial things.

Gandhi once said, "I like Christ very much for what he says, but I am so disappointed by Christians." And of course he did not mean that because they are human they are imperfect. But quite simply because they fail to live by the Word of their Lord. We are stagnant whilst the world expects so much from us. And God, I think would expect a lot from us. We do nothing of what we could do.

I will tell you a story from the Gerontiko about Saint Agathon, so you can understand better what I am talking about. Saint Agathon went to the market to sell some utensils. As he was walking down the street, he met a leper. The leper asked him "Where are you going?" "I am going down town to sell my utensils." "Take me with you, lift me up." So he lifts him onto his shoulders and they go down town together. When they reached their destination the leper said "Take me to the place where you sell your things" and Saint Agathon did as he was told. "How much did you sell that pot for?" asked the leper after the sale of the first pot. The Saint replied and the leper asked him to buy him a pie. So he did. When he sold the second piece, the leper asked again how much he sold it for and he asked him to buy another thing; so he did. The leper went on and on asking him to buy more things. He didn't allow Saint Agathon to keep any of the money he collected. This went on and on for a long time until the leper asked him "Do you have anything else to sell?" "No," he replied, "I have sold everything. And every penny I collected I gave it to you." The leper said, "Where are you going? Please take me back to the place where you found me. Could you do that?" Saint Agathon put him onto his shoulders and carried him back. When they reached the place, the leper said, "You are blessed, Agathon, both in heaven and on earth as you are a true man of God." And as soon as the saint looked towards him, the leper disappeared as he was an angel of god who wanted to test him.

Saint Agathon was a true man of God. I would never be able to behave like he did, I am embarrassed to say. I was thinking, for example, that if after I received my stipend for some function someone asked me to give him all the money I earned; I would certainly refuse, making up excuses. I sit down sometimes and think. How come some people in the past behave like true Christians, like human beings and we are unable to do so?

Another example I remember is Evergetinos, a monk who was given this name as he would help anyone who asked him. It means "benefactor" in Greek. You would say to him "Please help me move the bed in my bedroom as I cannot do it by myself", and he immediately ran to it; another person asked him to "please come to the garden ,help me dig a ditch to water the plants." and immediately he ran to it. Whatever he was asked to do he did with pleasure. Service, Sacrifice, Love. This is Christianity.

When I go to a monastery and an important person visits, I am touched by the monks who always do their best to welcome, him, guide him around, to speak to him and generally serve him. But most of all I am touched by the silent monks. They "disappear" early on although they too would have liked to see the important person, what he did, say, etc (it is only our common human tendency to be curious about anything considered unusual and special). On the contrary they make themselves scarce to prepare food and coffee and all the traditional welcoming treats for the guest, unseen and unsung in the kitchens. Yet, they began this paramount sacrifice of service, sacrifice, love and humility, following Christ. Christ is invisible, he does not appear, he is not heard. Humble people are the true Disciples of Christ; they are the ones who manage to experience the Gospel.

I have the same experience when I visit Mount Athos. Since I am a priest, monks serve me, concelebrate the Liturgy with me, invite me into their dining room and give me a seat of honour next to the abbot. All this makes me feel blessed. I must admit that I rarely give a thought for the "silent monks," the ones who are in the kitchen preparing food while I am in the church,........full of myself, selfish. These are the true Christians, the invisible monks. We are probably not willing to be like them.

A woman I once met said "Every Sunday I go to PIKPA in Voula helping kids with special needs. We help them get out of the car, we roll their wheelchairs, we help them to sit down, we go to the church, we assist them with receiving Holy Communion and finally we help them go back to their rooms." This is what I call unconditional solidarity, this woman is an invisible yet true Christian. All this takes time and effort. These are children requiring special care and extra love. Everything you do has to be guided by tender, loving care for their special needs. This is the example given and the love taught by our Lord Jesus Christ himself. "Do as I do. Whoever would be first should be last." Which one of us acts like this today? Which one of us Christians wants to be last? I don't remember myself being last ever. Yet these words are wise. Whoever wants to be first, needs to be last. Whoever wants to have authority, has to serve people, be a servant of all. Because the Lord blessed these, the least of his brethren.

I was touched by what this woman had to say about her voluntary work at PIKPA, especially when she said, "Every Sunday when we go to church with the kids, I really can't manage to listen to the preaching as the care of the children comes first." So I go to church a bit later to listen to the liturgy. Her heart was full of love, full of grace and God's mercy, although she doesn't have time to do what I do ,that is attend the full liturgy from before dawn. The difference is that I do indeed live in the pre-dawn darkness of sin, inconsistent between my preaching and deeds. That's what I think.

Another example which comes to my mind and gives a picture of what a real Christian is that of Saint Makarios. Once Saint Makarios went to the desert to visit an old monk. The monk thanked him warmly for his visit and invited him to his cell. "How are you, Father?" Saint Makarios asked. "I am very well, Thank God." "Is there anything I can do for you? Whatever you want, just ask for it." "What would I ask from you child?" the old man said hesitantly. "Just tell me, what would you like?" replied Saint Makarios, realising that the old monk had something else in mind, but was ashamed to ask. "Really...nothing, my child...I have been here in the desert for a long time and the only thing I need is dried bread." "What would you like me to bring to you next time I

Strengthen your Soul

come, father?" "I would love a small sesame bar. I've missed it. But I only give you a reply because you asked me. I don't really want anything. Saint Makarios replied, "I will be back in a minute." He left the cell and he kept walking for hours until he found a village where he could find a sesame bar. After a long time he returned and offered the sesame bar to the old monk. "But what have you done my dear child? I didn't mean anything when I said I missed the sesame bar." "You may have not meant anything but I couldn't resist bringing the bar for you."

I believe you understood what I was trying to say with this story, deeds are what counts, not just words. There is nothing symbolic in this. Saint Makarios put his feet where his mouth was. He walked a long distance to manage to get hold of the sesame bar. Was it possible that the monk's heart would not be full of gratitude after this move? Not to feel the love of Saint Makarios in his heart? I would probably have said, "A sesame bar? I will certainly bring one to you next time I come." And God knows when that would be, if ever. It would have appeared pointless to me to be running round the desert looking for sesame bars, in the middle of nowhere, where no one would see and praise such action. Isn't this the truth? Isn't this what has become of us?

Now listen to a similar story. One day someone was baking bread: hot, straight out of the oven, the whole place was filled with the smell. He therefore thought that it would be nice to send a loaf to a friend. But then he thought "Why should I get someone else to deliver it, it is best that I take it in person. It's a chance to sacrifice time to go and see him. I will make the effort." On his way, however, he tripped on a stone and his leg started to bleed. An angel of God then appeared to him, saying: "The steps you take for the love of Christ are not forgotten by God. You should know that nothing is wasted. God remembers everything." The man was so pleased with this announcement, forgot the bleeding, forgot the pain and thought, " Thank God for this. I did it out of love for my friend, and God will count this in my favour." He continued his walk and gave his friend the loaf.

The next day, he decided to repeat the good and godly deed by taking a loaf to yet another friend, a way to show him his love. When he was half way there, he met his friend coming towards him. Surprised, he asked, "Why did you come to find me? I wanted to bring you the loaf myself. You should have allowed me to do you this favour, I wanted to." And the other person said, "The door of Heaven is open to both of us. You went half way and I went the other half. Let's both make the effort and receive the reward from God." "I did not want you to put yourself out..."; "Neither did I, my friend...." and so on. The angel of God appeared once again and said, "This fight you just had is like sweet smelling fragrance in the eyes of God. These are the only quarrels God likes, as they are out of love."

Let's return to our own reality. Have you ever fought out of love? Have you ever had a fight with your wife because for example, she wanted to watch a particular series on TV while you wanted to watch something different? Did you ask for forgiveness because you were selfish, thinking only of your own needs? Did you back off, because you felt that her needs had priority over your own? Usually these quarrels end up with the couple watching two different programmes on two different TVs since neither wishes to put the other person's needs over theirs, refusing to make a sacrifice. Just imagine two people arguing over their holidays. "Let's go wherever you wish my love; let's go to your village and see your parents and relatives. We go to my parents all the time, it's time to see yours." "But what are you talking about, darling? Leave your mother all alone during the holidays?" "No, no, my love, we'll go to your village." They go on fighting out of love, refusing to sacrifice for each other. Isn't that wonderful?

Once I was invited to a church to celebrate the Holy Liturgy. There was a more senior, older priest who was the usual chief celebrant of the Divine Liturgy. As I was invited to celebrate and preach, he said to me, "Father, you be the chief celebrant today, I have been informed of the invitation extended to you by the church council. I will be vested beside you in the sanctuary." He didn't sound disappointed, on the contrary he meant what he said and graciously consented with a measure of relief, I thought. But I replied, "I will do the preaching when the time comes, Father, but please be the main celebrant." He went on refusing. He wouldn't have it. He was happy sitting next to me and not being the main celebrant of the Liturgy. At the end of the Holy Liturgy, he approached me saying, "Father, I was so happy concelebrating with you." I could see in his eyes that he was being genuine. Although he was senior to me and I didn't have the right to be main celebrant, he was not pretending, he showed true love. He was happy to take second place. I thought to myself, "God ,I want to be like him when I reach his age, to have true love inside my heart, to sacrifice for younger people and not ask to be the first and to have authority over other people." Even in church there is a hierarchy.

Where are all these examples? Are they part of our lives? Do we imitate them? Do we live like this? Personally, I don't think we can. The people who experience this are blessed. Why try and fight? People who manage to do this are worthy of respect and I am touched by their humility. We need to experience Christianity in practise, not in words. We need to experience Christianity even in the smallest details of our lives as this would be proof in deed that we may be hiding something great inside us. In this way, the truth is revealed in our lives.

Listen to a story about Saint Serapius Sendonius (= sheet). He received this sobriquet as his body was covered only by a sheet. Why was he covered by a sheet? Why did he give away all his possessions? Because he didn't want to own anything, not even a room or a house. Nothing. He loved other people so much that he gave them everything. Sometimes he used to sell himself as a slave to other people who needed help. He used to say to a friend, "Go and sell me as a slave to this house as there is need." So he did. The Saint lived in the house for two to three years according to their needs and with his kindness he managed to change their way of thinking, their heart. He softened their heart. They would say to him, "Why did you sell yourself as a slave? You are not a slave, you are our master, you are such a spiritual man, you have true love inside, the love of Christ." According to his "Life", he used to be deliberately reluctant at first to talk to his new 'masters' about Christ. He chose to show them a concrete example of Christian love that perplexed them at first but eventually led them to a practical understanding of Christ in the way he behaved and led his life. And after their conversion, when the time came for him to leave their service he returned the money they had paid for his indenture.

You can imagine what treasures these people hid in their heart, enabling them to behave and live like this. They possessed an inner strength and resilience. For, to be able to do all these things you need to have strength inside your heart, drawn from an unselfish happiness. These people did not suffer. They had a different source of strength inside their heart, so they didn't feel the deprivation of personal life. On the contrary, they felt the joy of making sacrifices for others. The joy given by our Lord, when we live the Gospel in our everyday life. Dear Lord, we experience the biggest miracle in our life. We need to understand some things. We need to understand that we have falsified your words. We argue over trivial changes in dogma ("Not an iota, not a jot....") but we forget that this is not all you said. You said some more practical things that we neglect in our day to day lives at our peril.

Perhaps, we as priests should worry most and live with a warning in our lives: "What will Christ say when we finally meet face to face? Do I know you?" It will really not matter what our excuses would be, how much we had done for Him. Christ was clear about what he asked of us but unfortunately he didn't see us practising all he said. He didn't see us wearing the apron as he did washing the Disciples' feet during the Last Supper. On the contrary, he sees each one of us appearing perfect, neat, decent, correct, but most of all hypocrites. We are fake. How are you going to show your love? How are you going to help your brother if you don't get down and get dirty with him? If you do not kneel in the dust and mud to wash his muddy feet? How are you going to make your brother happy if you don't sweat to go and bring him a small sesame bar?

This is what is being asked of us. Sacrifice. Contempt for our ego, and obscurity, living on the margin, a life that we have not chosen. All we ask for is glory, fame, a good name. What does Christ have to do with all this?

I feel that today I am repenting publicly for my behaviour. Everything that I have mentioned has to do with my own reality. Even today I declare that I have encountered holy men, Christians of today, parents, mothers, fathers, children, young people, experiencing the love of Christ. And I am stating clearly, with certainty that they exist. But I feel that I want to apologise for my own behaviour because I am afraid that when I finally meet my Lord he will say "I don't know you." You may well want to ask him, "How come you don't know him? He used to talk about you." He will say that my words were inconsistent with my deeds.

Perhaps you too should think about repenting, because repentance is not without a reason. Just think how many chances you had, you kicked them away without giving them a second chance, without making use of them and following them through. Just think of how many things the Lord asked you to do and you refused, finding excuses that had mostly to do with an overestimation of yourself. You shouldn't repent under emotional duress. You have to repent deeply, realising what you have done wrong, being able to correct your mistakes. Otherwise we remain people tied down by fancy ideas and emotions.

I thank you so much for bearing with me today. This is proof indeed that you are Christians, being patient and listening to your brother's mistakes. Even if he is a priest you have to accept his repentance and forgive him. I wish each one of us approaches Christ and takes advantage of every single opportunity he gives us. In this way we will be able to live the most beautiful miracle in our life which is the daily application of our Lords words, in our heart, body, soul and everyday life.

STUDY! STUDY!

Translation by Ioanna Alexaki

"So, I am no saint, unfortunately, but I try...I only have one son, K. and the only thing I ask for him of the Lord is that he knows Him. That he loves Him. He is a clever boy and a good pupil and everyone says that he is very mature and so on, but I don't care nor am I proud of that. Of course, this is also good, but the only thing I beg of Christ and His Holy Mother is that he worships the Lord. That's all I ask all day. I do not pressurise, I only give as much love as I possibly can, with my frequent errors, of course, but without judgement and murmur. Please wish that my child be blessed by God..."

T.P. Cyprus (e-mail)

Greetings dear listeners of the Church of Piraeus! Another week has passed and once again our programme 'Unseen Crossings' brings us close to each other. It is broadcast once a week, but that does not mean that we are close only once a week. I feel that we are close all week, because this one time when we have the programme, becomes the reason and the motive for us to think, to question, to occupy our minds with the things that we hear. It is also a reason to connect with one another and anticipation for our next meeting with one another. I look forward to meeting with you on the programme; you look forward to joining once again to listen. And the week flows by with our minds occupied with all the things we said on 'Unseen Crossings'.

What we do in church does not last only for that moment. It touches us. Then maybe you think that what you heard, what you received, has left, that you have forgotten it. But the seed that has fallen into your soul will start to work within you. It might take a while; God knows how much time it is going to be, maybe a few minutes, a few days, a few months. You will start to think about it, your mind will be occupied by it. All that you have heard will start gradually to work within you, many times even without you realising it. And I am really moved by those of you who come to me and tell me that they remembered at a later date things they had heard on the programme or during the sermon in church.

It is beautiful to listen and forget, and it is even more beautiful when what you have forgotten comes back to your mind, when you are reminded by God Himself, by the Holy Spirit. When He wakes you, and tells you: 'Remember what you once heard, in that sermon, in that speech. Remember what you read and at the time thought that it meant nothing to you and did not touch you. Now is the appropriate moment for you to be touched, for you to remember. Now that you need it, it will come to the surface.' And this is exactly what reveals the dynamics of the teachings of Christ, the truth in things, that something is true.

What do we mean when we say something is true? It is that which is not forgotten. *[In Greek, the word truth (αλήθεια pronounced "alythya") is derived from the word (λήθη pronounced "leethy") which means oblivion, forgetfulness and the negative prefix 'a' (pronounced as in arm).]* Truth is what is not forgotten. Maybe your mind forgets, but your heart doesn't. Your heart remembers and your heart will remind you when the time is appropriate.

As a small boy I used to go to Sunday school. I remember once a cousin of mine came from the village and that afternoon I had a meeting at Sunday school. So I was thinking whether to take him with me or not, because he did not know a lot about these things and I was embarrassed to tell him that I went to Sunday school. So I turned to an acquaintance of mine for advice on what I should do and he told me to take my cousin with me. I came up with the excuse that my cousin was not involved in these kinds of things, and because of that I did not know whether he was going to like it or not. But he said to me: 'It does not matter. Let him come. He will hear a couple of things that will enter his soul. He may forget them when he goes back to his village. But as time passes these things will work within him. Maybe even after years he may receive an answer within his soul, and remember nostalgically that evening's discussion. Most importantly he is going to remember the feeling of the atmosphere that touched him and the things that he received'.

So you see, it is not only the words, it is the whole atmosphere which enters into our soul when we are close to the church. It is what touches our hearts. It is God's grace which you do not know how it works, you do not know how it operates, but you can see the results. Like when you eat food. You may not be able to see the whole digestive procedure, how you digest, how you grow, how your cells renew, how all your systems operate in your body. What you see is that you are feeling well. What you see is that you have stamina, that you are strong and alive. You see that what you hear, what you take in, either as food or as knowledge gives you strength and stamina in life, so that you can endure and go on. And that is the proof that the words that you heard were not random or transient words, but were divine words.

These words may have come out of an earthly mouth, out a sinful human – because as Father Justin Popovich used to say, we are all sinners, others less and others more, but we are all big sinners, and I am not excluding myself – but despite the fact that the words may have come out of the lips of these sinners, they are fermented by God and with the Grace of God, and these words enter into your kind heart, your generous heart, your well-intended, thirsty heart and then they bring about results. That is the beauty of it. You are the one who is going to perform the miracle, along with these poor words.

Some of you have told me that my words caused them to think, touched them. Somebody told me once: 'Since I heard what you had said about the Holy Bible, I wanted to thank you. I had been reading the Holy Bible, but I never studied it regularly. However, when I heard you talk about that issue it made me think more, it occupied my mind, it touched me and since then I read the Holy Bible more often'. What I have to say to this person is that this achievement is due to his honest, well- intended and thirsty soul. He heard some words from me and that caused his soul to work with the Grace of God, to brew and to achieve this beautiful result.

It is very touching to realise how people benefit from what they hear in the Church of Piraeus, whether they listen to the programme regularly, or randomly once in a while. They are moved and touched by the words, the teachings, the comments, the explanations of the Holy Gospel, the hymns, the psalms, the descriptions of the journeys to Mount Athos and to Jerusalem, the opinions of everyday people, the explanations of the fathers of the church, theologians, literature teachers and scientists. These words touch their souls.

I was once so moved by a listener who contacted us to tell us that she listened to us every night. (Our programme is repeated at night) Why was this person listening at night?

She worked in a nursing home taking care of old people and she was working during the night. So the programme keeps her company while she is working helping her fellow humans, and through that she is helped also. I was moved when I realised that there are people who listen to our programme during the night and benefit. This is one of the beautiful things that the church offers.

Many times I think that we live in a beautiful era. There may be a lot of negative elements, but if we make proper use of these elements we can really understand the beauty that is hidden. Father Paisios (Pa-ee-sios) used to say that God takes the mess He sees in our lives and turns it into carpets that lead to heaven. God intervenes and blesses the problems of our era, makes them holy, giving us different perspectives. Our era is a very beautiful era. Maybe today there is an excess of sin, but at the same time there an overabundance of the grace of God. There may be a lot of terrible things happening, but there are still people who love holiness, who cherish prayer, who long to dedicate their lives to Christ, through the family they will have, through the children they will have, even through their jobs and tasks. They are people with clear faith, clear goals and purposes, people who read spiritual books.

We live in a very beautiful era, from the point of view of what is offered on the spiritual level. We have a lot of potential. Those of you who are adults, fifty or sixty years old, remember back when you were young. Were there so many possibilities in the spiritual and church life? No! In previous years people did not have so many spiritual opportunities and horizons. Today there are radio stations, books, and passages written by the fathers of the church, unbelievably wonderful publications with so much meaning and significance that touch the soul. Today we live in such an era, which God blesses and helps us obtain strength so that we can endure our problems. He helps us draw strength and have stamina to endure any problems that may come in the future, maybe on a global scale.

So the church cannot be dealing with the darkness and all the things that are not right, the church cannot be digging into the filthiness of the world. The church has a proposition. The church presents the truth to you, gives you light and health, and gives you what is right, true and pure. And then you take it. As soon as you touch the light that is provided for you, and let it enter within you, the darkness will leave automatically. Besides, what is the point in dealing with what is bad in the world, with the panic of our times? The only thing we will achieve is to become part of this whole procedure and become ill as a result of all this. This is not the solution. The solution is to live in our own beautiful world, in the world of the church which is the world of truth.

I tell you these things because this is the way I feel about these things also. I would like to say to our friends who have expressed the wish to meet with me in person that a lot of times it is easier to listen to someone and process what he is saying instead of meeting him in person. Because you may have high expectations of this person and when you meet him you may get disappointed because he may prove that he was not who you thought he was. And that applies to me as well. It is better to listen to a couple of things from a person instead of asking too much of him, because he may not have more to offer. I admit that I do not have more to give you than the few things I say and a 'Lord have mercy' that I will say during Holy Mass. And that is only because God is there, and the sacred holiness of Christ is channelled through me, it works, and God listens to your prayer and helps you.

However, I have a suggestion to make because some people consider it necessary to tell me something in person. So if any of you wants to say something and wants to communicate with me, then you can write a letter to the radio station, to the Church of Piraeus, to the programme 'Unseen Crossings.' You may feel the need to express your pain, your sorrow in writing, you may want to ask a question, you might have an issue that you would like to discuss and would like to receive an answer through our radio programme at some point. The address is: No 47, Deligiorgi Str. Post code 18534, Piraeus.

I like the letters of the people that express something personal, that mention something that has touched them, or hurt them, or felt joy that they want to share with us. What they say teaches us too. I feel that I am taught more than I teach. I think about things, I benefit, I count on you. That is why I thank all those who have already sent me letters and cards. I specifically remember a letter from a woman named Loukia. She wrote simply to express her pain and she moved me because she wrote that she was not asking for anything. She simply wanted to tell me that 'Father we are together. We are Christians and I simply want to share this joy of communication, of love and unity.' She just wanted to tell me that we both belong to Christ and she asked for nothing else except for me to pray for her, for us to pray for one another.

I like a lot the people who are humble in their problems. And while they may be drowning in problems, they make no demands, they just want to talk about their suffering to someone, to share their pain with someone and then to silently go on with their lives. They make no demands. They make no complaints. They do not claim happiness. They wait for God's will. They wait for God to give them something better.

I remember how much I was moved when I received a phone call from another woman who told me: 'Father, it does not matter if you do not talk to me. What I listen to on your programme will give me the answers. This is what I wanted to tell you. I am not worthy. I do not want you to get tired because of me.' I would like to say that this woman is worthy; she should not feel that way. You are all worthy. And it is not me who is saying this; it is God, because He knows how much each and every one of us is worthy, which is why he is concerned with us, personally. And He is concerned with our lives, with our souls, to support us and to help us.

This is what I wanted to say as an introduction, and at this point I would like to mention again the issue of parents and their relationship with their children. I believe that the subject is inexhaustible. It is a vital issue, an endless issue that all of us are preoccupied with. I would like you to know that there can never be a speech or a lecture that will provide solutions to your problems, nor is it a subject whose content can be fully covered. Because, within the family life, one is always learning, from when one starts and meets somebody, gets into a relationship, gets engaged, gets married and has children, until the end of one's life. And maybe it does not stop even then. Being a parent does not stop when your life ends, but it continues forever, because even in eternity you will continue the task of helping your children and the entire world.

So I would like to plead with you and to give you some very friendly advice. It would be very good if parents at home did not keep telling their children: 'Study! Study!' pressuring them about their school and their tutoring. There is pressure, there is oppression, and there is tension which is absolutely justifiable within the framework of what is good and appropriate. Many parents have rightfully expressed their query: 'But father, mustn't my child study? Mustn't my child learn good manners? Shouldn't my child learn to get dressed in time? Shouldn't my child get ready to go to school?' concerning younger children. 'Mustn't they come home early?'

I agree with the fact that all these concerns that you have as parents show deep interest and love for your children and it goes without saying that you are not asking for anything irrational, unreasonable or bad. It is good and right for you to want your child to study, to get dressed properly and not to go out without taking a jacket, to come home at an appropriate time, because you are concerned and you worry that something bad might happen. However, all these 'shoulds' and 'musts' and the way parents inflict them on their children, a lot of times, cause tensions and quarrelling in the home. Indeed, all these things are appropriate, it would simply be better if we were careful about the way we express them. Our children should not feel their relationship to us as torture. It is not torture. Knowledge, studying, whatever you ask your children to do, is and should be the fruit of love; the fruit of inspiration and enthusiasm, and you must help your children understand that.

Can you help your children become so enthusiastic that they will choose to study without any pressure from you? Can you help your children learn to love studying and learning, to love beauty, to love order and tidiness in their life? Can you help them in such a way that it is by their own choice that they are composed, fulfilled, authentic human beings and to strive to achieve these things? This is where the beauty lies, in having the eagerness to do all these things. Maybe even your children will admire what you are doing. This is even more amazing.

I would like to share with you something from my own soul. When I was a young boy, in the second grade of primary school, I stopped watching television. Even today I watch very little television and I would like to tell you how this came to happen. Well, up to the age of seven I used to watch a lot of television, almost continuously. Back then of course there were not so many channels, there were only two, but that was not a problem for me! I knew the whole programme by heart! This habit of mine was a cause of a lot of arguments at home. Very often there was not enough time left for me to study and do my homework for school for the next day. However, strangely enough, it had not affected my grades at all, I was a very good student, so I was satisfied and I used to say that everything was fine. My parents, however, wanted me to study, to rest, to sleep more. They wanted to watch something on television, which was impossible, since I had occupied it! Many times they would carry me to bed because I was stuck in front of the television and I would not move away!

So one day, my school teacher asked me to tell my mother to come to school in order to congratulate her. The reason was that I could count from two to twenty, counting all the even numbers and back. Two, four, six, eight, ten, twelve etc. – and back – and I could do that very quickly while the other children could not. So my mother came to the school and while she was being congratulated by the teacher and I was feeling like I was going to burst from pride and ego, my mother said to the teacher: "You praise him, but let me tell you how much trouble he causes at home. He watches television all day long, he doesn't stop not even for a moment, from the moment the programme begins till the moment it ends, he is there, staring at the screen (back then, the programme started in the afternoon and finished a little after midnight). So my husband and I are fighting and quarrelling with him and with each other about this situation.'

In that moment, and without me expecting it, the teacher turned and slapped me on the cheek very hard! I did not know what to do, how to react! One moment I was happy and full of bliss by the praise I was getting and the pride I was feeling, and the next my lips started to tremble and I wanted to cry! The embarrassment I felt was unbelievable. I became red in the face, my ego was injured, and I was ridiculed. I felt very badly about what had happened. When we left, my mother was holding my hand so I squeezed her hand and said to her: 'I am never going to bring you to school again! I asked you to come to listen to praise, and you ridiculed me. Did you have to say all these things to the teacher?' That was the first event which happened in primary school.

Then, when I went to the first grade of junior high school, I was impressed by the fact that, unlike primary school where we had the same teacher for all the lessons, we had a different teacher for every subject. I was very impressed, I liked very much the fact that I was meeting new people, new teachers. That lifted my morale and increased my interest. The teacher who triggered my interest more was my Maths teacher. He had a very beautiful and attractive way; I could say an impressive way, of explaining everything. So one day he was explaining the plus and minus signs. I was so happy that I had understood! I got home around seven o'clock in the afternoon, because I had an afternoon shift, and I thought that it would be a good idea to solve the exercises I had for homework then because the information was fresh in my mind. However, the problem was that my favourite television programme started at eight. So, with a lot of stress and looking constantly at my watch, I started solving my exercises. Time passed without my realising it, since I was so absorbed into what I was doing, I was so enthusiastic. As soon as I solved the first exercise, I turned to the back of the book, to the answers section, to verify my answer. The solution of the exercise was correct! I was thrilled! But I had three more exercises. I looked at my watch and the time was five minutes to eight. 'I've got enough time, I can do it', I thought, because I could not get television out of my mind! So I began solving the next exercise and as soon as I finished, I checked, this too was correct! The first thing I thought was that mathematics was a wonderful subject and I had started to love it! But at that time, I heard from the living room the theme music of the programme I wanted to watch! It was beginning! I was getting ready to get up from the chair, to go to the living room, but I threw a quick glance at the next exercise and suddenly I found myself immersed in trying to solve that one too! In the beginning I couldn't solve it and so I looked at the next chapter hoping to understand what I had to do and I got completely absorbed until I managed to solve it! Last thing I remember was hearing the closing credits. My programme had ended! The time was a few minutes to nine, time had passed without me realising how. In the beginning I was sad, but then I sat and thought and I found the answer within myself: 'It doesn't matter, wasn't what you did better? Wasn't it beautiful that you solved your Maths exercises and you were so happy with what you did? You did it out of love, out of desire. I don't want to see that programme again. I will do exercises. I will read books.'

I think that all that happened was probably from God. And since then, truly, because I fell in love with what I was doing,

I fell in love with studying; I never watched television again through all my school years, junior high school, senior high school, and university. Much later, after my thirties I began to watch selectively a few things, and I did that because I wanted to keep somewhat in touch with the world and the reality of life.

Of course with this attitude I went to the other extreme, which is not the best thing to do. I remember at home my parents telling me: 'Ok, we told you not to watch too much television, but that is too much! Come and sit with us for a little while in the living room!' And I would say to them: 'I will come and sit with you. But turn off the television so we can talk, have a discussion. I don't want to watch television. It had become an addiction for me for so many years and now that I am free of that addiction, I want to relax. Leave me alone, I want to study'. I tell you the truth, my beloved, no one taught me this, nobody told me 'don't watch television' using arguments to convince me. This need emerged from my soul, because in its place I found something more beautiful, something more attractive that charmed my soul, beautified my inner world and I loved it.

I fell in love with reading and studying. This is what love is about, to love something with all your heart so that you can find the strength and the will to let go of something that you do in order to replace it with something else, something new. And nobody can make you do this, if you do not want to, if you do not feel this warmth in your soul. The word love within the church means intense passion. It is not connected only with issues of the flesh, but generally with passion, with enthusiasm. When they call someone an 'enthusiast' it means that this person loves what they are doing. Life cannot move forward without love. If you do not love, if you haven't fallen in love with whatever it is that you are doing, then you will not prosper. You will not have results, because you are not happy with what you are doing. That is why, whatever you choose to do in your life you must love it, do it with enthusiasm and joy.

I chose to become something in my life, because I could not imagine that I could become something different. Whatever they told me to prevent me from becoming a theologian was not enough to make me deviate from what I had already decided, because I loved it from the bottom of my heart. So when I finished junior high school, I indicated that I wanted to go to the theoretical branch of senior high school so I could enter and study Theological Studies at University. As soon as my Math teacher learned about my decision he was surprised and told me that it wasn't possible because I had such good grades in the science subjects (19 out of 20 in Maths, 20 out of 20 in Physics etc), how could I give up on those grades and become a theologian! So he started presenting me with a lot of arguments to change my mind, he said things like a teacher of theology will not find work easily in a school, that I would have a brilliant career in something else, but I remained stable with my views. I told him that I was not interested in anything else and that I wanted to get involved in humanitarian studies, because I wanted to be in contact with people and not through Maths. I wanted a more personal relationship with people and as a theologian I would accomplish what I desired. My Maths teacher called even the teacher's association of the school to tell them that they should not let me go, but I had made my decision and I did exactly what I wanted to do and I never regretted it. Despite the fact that I was still immature because I was a young boy then, I knew what I wanted to do. I wanted what I was going to follow in the future to be something I would wake up in the morning and be happy to do, and not a drudgery and something I would force myself to do. And I also knew that I did not want my motive to be either the money nor the salary.

Never do anything in your life that will keep you on your feet only for the salary. Because somewhere along the line it will break your soul, you will get tired. Do you want to become something? Do it. Even if you choose the strangest thing, if you love it, you will succeed and you will thrive and prosper in the field that you have chosen, contrary to someone who might be doing the same thing as you without loving it.

So, I went ahead with a lot of hope, faith and enthusiasm for what I had chosen to do and in the end I succeeded. And another thing which is great is that I got employed in a public school as a teacher of theology, which was quite difficult, and now that I wake up every morning and go to school, I say to my students: 'Choose something in your life that when the time comes for you to go to work, you will be happy that you are doing it. Whether you work in the public sector, or in an office, or a factory, whether you work in a garage or a construction site, it is important that you wake up in the morning and feel happy and fulfilled with what you chose to be.' There are people who are happy about their job. I know some guys who are working in their father's ironmongery and are very happy, because it had always been their inner drive. They are very skilled with their hands. They love their job. It gives them satisfaction and fulfilment. They want to take raw material and give it different shapes. I know, for example, a plumber who comes to my house and I consider him a university professor due to his usefulness in my life! I need him! I value him very highly, because he loves what he does, and he does it with zest and enthusiasm. He is never anxious. I watch him and I get sick because I know that what he does I could never bear to do, I could never do it, because it does not suit me!

So every person must find what suits them, what they love to do. Then I became a priest and I chose priesthood because I knew it would fill me with joy, it would fill my soul with happiness. And when I think back, I do not regret my decision, on the contrary, I rejoice in my choice and I thank God. It is beautiful not to regret things that you did, decisions that you made. I do not regret for loving Christ, theology, and school. I regret nothing. It is very beautiful to be able to say: 'If I was ever born again, I would do the same thing.'

What I chose to do was not because of any imperative need, but because I myself wanted it. I did not leave things to chance either. For example, I did not get into the school of Theology just because I happened to fill in the application, or because I had no other choice. Sometimes, even if someone gets into a specific school by chance, they may end up liking what they do. I knew somebody who had passed into Agricultural studies because he did not manage to get the grades he needed to get into the school he preferred, however, he ended up loving what he was doing. He loved the science, the land, the diversity of plants and flowers, and the wisdom with which God created all these things. However if he had not managed to like it I do not know if he should have continued. If he had not liked it maybe he should have looked for something else that he would have fallen in love with, something he would enjoy doing in his life and be good at.

I do not know if it is proper to say that some people are not suited for family life. Some people should not start a family, because it is not right for them. They do not do it with love, devotion or enthusiasm; they do not love it, they do not start with the appropriate preconditions. I do not know what may be the reasons that force people to get married, maybe pressure from their families, maybe fear of being alone. Anyway, they expect to find certain things in the marriage, they find other things and in the end they get disappointed and they break up. I have had numerous discussions with women who are disappointed in their marriages – and I am not mentioning these things to criticise anyone, but to use examples to help you all realise the situations I mention. Many times women (and men, of course) come to me and tell me that they wake up in the morning and they weep because of the disappointment in their life. 'I do not like the life I am living. I do not like the path I have chosen' 'Which path did you choose?' 'I do not mean that I am alone, I simply do not like the fact that I started a family. I think of my children, my house, my chores and I weep! I have withered, I feel depressed, and I have lost myself!' 'Why did the beauty, the sparkle leave your soul? Why is it lost? That which keeps you alive?' And do you know what most of them reply? 'It is not lost. It simply was never there in the first place. I did not set off with enthusiasm. I did not set off with love.

I like this word 'love' because it expresses great truths and strong, divine relationships. Love of God, love of humans. It means to be able to love and to give. And so you manage in that way. I have seen mothers with many children, who have so many things to do, and despite that they do not have enough money to support their family and their home the way they would like to, they have so much joy and enthusiasm for what they do that they never give up. And you see them and you ask yourself: 'How can this woman do all that?' The answer is simple. It is because she loves what she does, she is in love with what she does and she is enthusiastic about what she does and while her body might get tired, her soul is not. And while she gives everything, she rejoices. And she lives what is written in the Psalms (Psalm

102, verse 5, according to the Greek version, 103, verse 5, according to the English version): 'so that your youth is renewed like the eagle's.' She is like the eagle that flies high, soars to the clouds traversing the skies with her liveliness. That is how these women view life. And as the years pass, they do not get ill, they do not wither, or lose their morale, and their spirit never sinks. Instead, their soul gets sweeter and more beautiful. The strength of your body may one day leave you, but the livelihood of your soul should never leave from within you, no matter how old you are.

Maybe I said too much in my attempt to conclude what I started saying. It is very important not to tell our children: 'Study! Write! Do this! Do that!' all of these things that we tell them they should do in such an oppressive way. We should not be giving orders or instructions. You yourself must become an example for your child and show through your actions what is useful and beneficial, 'illustrate' it through your own life. Your child then sees you and may envy what you are doing, admire what you are doing. I met teachers, preachers, theologians, priests who were a source of inspiration for my life. I admired those people, because I envied, I loved what they were doing and the passion with which they were doing it. It was as if I was drunk, and when you are drunk you move forward and you do not know what you are doing. When you get drunk with something you love, you do not operate with your reason, you operate with your heart. And the reason of the heart is wonderful and whatever you desire to do you succeed and you make it happen.

Proof of all that I have mentioned so far is my own life, my present life. I am glad, I rejoice in the things that I chose to do, the school, the radio programme, the confession, with all the things that I do in the church, because it is what I always wanted to do in my life to give my life meaning. I am not right, I am not perfect, or infallible, but the field that I chose to work on and cultivate, I am glad that I chose it because it is what suits me, and it is where I work doing the best I can.

So it is beautiful for the children to become inspired, to become enthusiastic with whatever they want to undertake and we should not try to make them, to force them to do it by shouting at them. The mistake is primarily ours, because we do not give our children a role model, an example which they will envy, which will charm them and that they would want to imitate. As we read in the Apolytikion (introit) of the Feast of the Holy Pentecost, 'Blessed are You, O Christ our God, who made fishermen all-wise, by sending down upon them the Holy Spirit, and through them, drawing all the world into Your net.' They charmed the world, and like a net, they drew everyone near. How? There was flame and liveliness in what they were doing.

Television today is a very bad example for the children, because it makes them get enthusiastic with things that are sinful, phony, without quality, without authenticity or ethics. It does not provide them with strong truths in order to be able to stand on their own feet in their life. This is why children today do not have dreams, do not have ideals. Or their ideals are purely technological, materialistic, like for example, knowledge of computers and its progress. These things fascinate children but they do not provide them with quality of life.

So this is the point where we should ask ourselves. In our homes, are we such an example of inspiration? A lot of parents think that they are not appropriate role models because they are not educated enough because they might have gone only to primary school and not to university. But you do not need to be educated for your child to admire you, for you to be a source of inspiration regarding your stance in life! You only need to be able to narrate a beautiful story, to show your children that life is beautiful, that it has quality. That life is a place where we are going to know and experience God, to learn to love. We must teach our children to be humble and to have a beautiful soul. We must teach them that it is worth fighting to live and not to make money. We are the ones who are going to guide our children how to learn to love beauty, to coexist with their loved ones and to seek knowledge to enlighten their minds to understand the world. Through knowledge they will understand the value of humility and they will praise God for that. Their soul will be cleansed and they will find serenity in their hearts. In this way they will be able to see clearly what they want, what they really like and follow it.

Children today are confused, I could even say ill. We have made them ill, involuntarily. Through all those hours of concentration in front of a television set or a computer screen they have come to know brutality, harshness, violence, they have flattened every value that would shape the morality of their soul. It is reasonable, as a result to have abnormal behaviour, nervousness, tensions because they feel inadequate to respond to the mire of this society and this life.

But when the family is balanced, when it is a Christian family which is serene like a protected harbour then the children will receive the correct stimuli and role models. In such a family there is no need to talk too much; the beautiful environment and the purity penetrate effortlessly in their souls.

I remember the example of a priest who was married and had many children. They had chosen not to have a television set in their house. However, they had a piano and other musical instruments, because they considered music as very good to the education of the souls of their children. Also, they had distributed all the housework, something like the 'common work' that the monks do in the monasteries. One time I happened to be there when they were preparing green beans for their meal! Since they were so many, they had shared the work so they would finish more quickly. As soon as they finished they all sat around the piano and started to sing! One was playing the piano, another was playing the flute, they were singing and clapping their hands, generally it was a very beautiful and joyful atmosphere, full of love and warmth. This was followed by board games and the whole afternoon passed with laughter and teasing! So this priest was telling me that every time he asks his children if they want him to buy them a television set they consider it absolutely irrational! They tell him: 'What do we need it for? We have a lovely time just the way we are, don't we?', and he feels very satisfied with this situation because he feels the strong bonds that his family has and he considers that the souls of his children keep the purity of their age. It is a fact that when a child is having a good time he or she does not want to watch television. When a child has a good time with whatever he or she is doing, they do not want to change that with anything.

So today our children do not have inspiration, they do not like what they are doing and that is why they do not do it well. So do not have the habit of always scolding the child, because sometimes the responsibility might be somebody else's, the teacher's, the priest's, an adult's, somebody who has promised to be a source of inspiration for the children and is not. When for example, the child has a teacher in school who does not love his or her profession, who is bored and does the lesson as if it is a burden, a teacher who chose to become a teacher not out of love for teaching, but because it gave him or her a salary and three months vacation in the summer, a teacher who is counting the years till pension time, then why would you scold your child because he or she does not do well in that lesson? Why don't you think that somebody may not have taught the lesson properly, that maybe they did not help the child to understand or they were unable to trigger the child's interest because they did not know how to make the lesson interesting?

I believe that many teachers do their work well. The teacher always explains the lesson. But this is not what makes the student understand. What matters is for the lesson to be taught in a loving environment, so that the child will feel that and become interested. When the child grows to love the lesson, then the concepts are understood more easily and they even move on without even realising that. They might ask questions about concepts they have not been taught yet because the mind is working charged by enthusiasm and bears opinions and ideas. It conceives ideas.

However, this is not how things are today. School is not like that. Our educational system is not like that. There is no enthusiasm for teaching nor for learning and the only thing we are enthusiastic for is, maybe, to go on strike and occupy the school buildings. The teachers have lost their strong desire, their love for their work, at least most of them because there are certainly exceptions and I do not want to be unfair to those. But wherever there is enthusiasm the children will respond. That is why, my dear parents, we must know how to interpret someone else's behaviour appropriately and shouting at our children is not always the solution.

When the child gets enthusiastic about something he or she will stop whatever they were doing if it was somewhat meaningless, and didn't give any quality to their life. When children spend endless hours on their computer that means that there is nothing better for them to do, nothing else that would excite them enough to want to do it. One day a student told me at school, when I asked him to tell me a complaint that he had about life: 'My complaint is that I have to sleep. I would like it better if we did not need to sleep'. I asked: 'Why'? And he replied in all honesty: 'So I can play on my computer all night! I feel very sad when I have to go to bed.' Imagine the love this child has for that thing, it had stolen his heart! Like the monks at Mount Athos who do not want to sleep out of their love for God and so they stay up all night awake and they pray; this child behaves in the same way with his computer! This is why this is similar to a theological statement: 'I wish there was no sleep, so I can live what I love'.

This child – and certainly he is not the only one – loved something, he just did not love the right thing because no one gave him alternative options, no one showed him a different path. There are things that you can instil, inspire in another person, things you can teach your child. We can teach these things if we are willing. You can't have as a constant excuse, whenever you get home from work that you are tired and you do not have the time or the energy to spend with your child. Your child needs you. Your child needs and must be inspired by you. It is not right to send your child to watch television or to sit at their computers for hours so you can relax. You must talk to your children, discuss with them. Nor is it appropriate if the only thing you do, the only way you communicate with your children is by shouting at them and sending them to their room to study. In that way we give them the wrong message, we show them that we have other directions and other goals. Therefore when you want your child to progress and succeed, you must not shout, you must not demand, but mainly you must pray for that. Pray and show them the beauty of what you are suggesting. Explain it to them. Beauty will move them, beauty always touches and moves.

Once I went to buy a book, a version of the original Homer's Odyssey that had a parallel translation from Ancient to Modern Greek. The reason was that Mr. Ganotis had sent me as a gift a very remarkable book he had written with comments about the Odyssey and I wanted to buy the original so I could comprehend the comments while reading the ancient text. In the bookshop where I went, I was looking at different publications in order to find the one that would move me, I wanted it to be well written and translated so I would be challenged to read it. Beauty always attracts you to things and urges you to get involved.

The same thing happens with children. When you show them something beautiful they will want to go near. Father Paisios says: 'When the eyes of the children sparkle from the love of Christ they will leave everything else'. The holy men, the saints left everything and devoted themselves only to Christ. They were no longer attracted to women, pleasures, food, delights, perfumes, money or possessions. Despite the fact that they were promised numerous things, much more beautiful – maybe on the surface – than what they were experiencing, they replied that they had loved the most magnificent thing and they were serving it and that they were even willing to die for it. The beauty of a woman, the tastiness of food, the pleasure of money and glory did not touch or move them because they were in love with something much higher. And that love that they felt conquered everything. So the saints through their martyrdom, suffered as humans, they were in a lot of physical pain, but their soul was experiencing situations that cannot be described, because we cannot understand them. We have not touched that love which erases, cancels all other things. We have not been charmed by that beauty which is going to make us look at all the other beauties differently and place them in a different place in our hearts. What happens today is that we give priority to things that should not have priority in our lives, but this is the way we have learned to do. It makes sense, however, since we have not yet seen the beauty of the truth, the beauty of God, since we have not yet been charmed by Him.

Nevertheless, things do not change by force or violence or shouting. Do not ask others to do things that they cannot do, or transcend situations just because you are asking them to. Transcending, overcoming a situation and living something else require the presence of charm, attraction, admiration and love. And this love and admiration do not come as a result of being shouted at or with demands, but with prayer. If you love Christ and the beauty of what you are doing in your life, if you love the world, God and human beings, and this is something grand that you have to offer, then the others will feel it in their own soul also and will want to imitate you, to follow your example, because your serenity will fascinate them.

This is exactly what will happen in your child's soul also. If your children see that their father and mother do not have tensions between them, that they do not shout at them, that they do not try to touch their souls with harsh hands and words like thorns, that they come to them in a gentle way, then they will listen and will not react. It is very beautiful for a child to have two parents who love each other, who are in love with everything that is beautiful in this world, who have beautiful inspirations. Because it is then that the child's soul will unblock. And if the miracle does not happen now, be sure that it will happen at some other time. Surely, many of you will tell me: 'Yes, but if my child does not study now that he should, then it is going to be late. If what you are saying happens after fifteen years, what then? He will have finished school and he will have achieved nothing.' I would agree with you up to a point, but I will tell you again that we cannot do anything by force; the child cannot mature before the appropriate time, we cannot force anything to mature before its time. God has His own ways. God has His own schedule, His own plan for every human being. If the tactic you have followed so far has failed, or fails constantly, ask yourselves whether you must think of something else and find another way.

Those things I am talking to you about, I do not demand that you do them because then I will be doing the same mistake I am advising you to avoid. I am just trying to make you question some things, ask yourselves, think whether the tactics we use sometimes in order to pressure others to make them change, the fact that we shout at our children to make them study, is not the correct one and we should find a way that will touch their heart. We want our children to do their homework and study their lessons because the trigger and the enthusiasm have been given from the heart, and because God's love and touch will help them.

Maybe I am wrong too and I may seem to exaggerate, so I ask you to forgive me. I am not a parent, I do not have children. In the end it is you who experience your everyday life. If you have any suggestions, write to the address I mentioned earlier. I will be happy to receive your letters. I simply would like my words to cause you to think, to question and help you see things from another point of view, from another perspective, because life is never a one-way track. I wish you all a loving and warm environment in your homes. I wish you all to seek the truths of the knowledge of God so that you can show these truths easily and beautifully to your children so that they get to know them, because the truth of Christ is the source and the basis of all knowledge.

May God be always with us!

LORD, SOFTEN MY SOUL

Translation: Ioanna Alexaki

"Hello, Father. I am L. from K. and with my mother E. we listen to your homilies, which help us to a great extent! At present, I want to write so many things, but the most important is that I suffer from multiple sclerosis. Thanks to God I try to accept it fully and get over it... It is not easy, but I also have my mother who helps me...We listen to your homilies and we thank you for them. Please pray that my heart softens from within the tribulations that I am going through..."
L.B. Mytilene (e-mail)

And what about me, my Christ, how am I to blame? How is it my fault, for example, that many times my heart is like land, dry? Like the arid field, the barren field, that does not accept the seed within it. That nothing can sprout within it? But, can you blame the field? Can you scold it? Can you say to a field «why are you like that? »

There are a lot of times when a person feels bored with no apparent reason. One feels bored and does not want to pray, bored and does not want to go to church. He or she does not want to listen, or listens and then immediately forgets. So, is it my fault that I listen and forget? Is it my fault that I do not feel like reading spiritual books, texts written by the Fathers of the church? «This is how the land of the soul is», you might say.

I say all this, my beloved friends, motivated by the parable of the sower and everything that Christ teaches us through that parable, all that He reveals to us about the human souls.

There was a farmer once who went out to sow his field. While he was sowing, some of the seeds fell on the path and were wasted, because they were stepped on by people who were passing by or were eaten by the birds. Other seeds fell on stones and as soon as they sprang up a little, immediately they became yellow and dried, because there was neither enough soil nor humidity to help them grow. Some seeds fell among thorns which choked the sprouts. Finally, some of the seeds fell on fertile ground and so they grew producing hundredfold grain.

So, look though this parable at how many kinds of people there are.

Our Christ describes, in just a few lines, all human souls. The seed is the Word of God and the places where the seeds fell are the different kinds of people who accept the Word according to their intention to let it grow or not. The people who are symbolised by the path are those who may listen to the Word of God, but who cannot believe in order to be saved. The stones are those who do not have spiritual roots and so abandon the effort as soon as the first difficulty appears, while the thorns symbolise those who choke in the material goods and riches, and as a result they push the Lord's teachings to the side. Finally, the fertile land symbolises the virtuous souls whose hearts are open to God, who listen and carefully keep His words, making them give fruit.

So, you come and you ask me: How is it my fault for being the way I am? Can you scold a field because it has got thorns or, on the contrary, can you praise it because it is fertile? Did the field do anything to make this happen? You might tell me that you would really like to do a lot of things, like going to church, and reading the books written by the Fathers but that you cannot bring yourself to do these things, it is not something that you love, and as a result you become bored. You tell me that you do not believe all these things and that you are not touched by them; so, it is very suitable for you to ask me if it is your fault.

I think that initially, it is not your fault for being the way you are. Because a human being, my beloved, is not an island in the world, an island isolated from the rest of the world. We are united, we are connected to one another, we live close to each other and we are directly affected by our surroundings, by the people around us, by the beliefs of the society and the times we live in, and other more general components. Each one of us may have an internal disposition, but his or her soul is subject to some alterations, good or bad, depending on the different influences. So you understand that what you are is the result of many factors. When, for example, you see someone who has an inclination towards spiritual life, who loves spiritual life and the soil of his heart thirsts for spirituality, do not be quick to say that this is a good, decent person, because you do not know the preconditions that this person had. Maybe this good person should have been even better, based on the preconditions of his or her life. And while you admire this person, God may consider that he lacks a lot more. And maybe on the other hand, while you see yourself as someone who is lazy, slow, and living in spiritual lethargy, God may be praising you to His angels saying that you have accepted a few drops from His divine rain despite the fact that you had no help and lived in a very difficult home, family and work environment, you have made the most of what He gave you. So God grades you differently.

God does not use the same criteria to evaluate people. It is impressive, how in the parable of the sower, Christ compares the land of our world to the land of our soul. Christ does not criticise. He does not scold anyone. He does not make any remarks. He simply observes and describes. Why does He describe? To tell us that «I, as God Almighty, I know you». He knows how our soul operates; He knows who of us have true passion in our hearts and who are being lazy, who are choking and who are blossoming patiently. He observes us and leaves the rest to us. He simply wants us to be in awe in the face of the reality of salvation, of spiritual fruition! And He tells us His parables to keep us vigilant, aware.

We must sit by ourselves and think where each one of us belongs, what is the condition of our souls, to become aware of our real situation and see our true self, how we are on the inside. Do you like spirituality? Does your soul thirst? You think, not much. You think you are like one of these people who whatever they hear comes in one ear and goes out the other. Those people who do not question anything, those who do not think that what they hear might concern them. Are you like that? Or do you belong to the other category of people whose souls rejoice when they hear something beautiful? Are you an enthusiastic person, an optimist who believes that you can achieve anything and everything, but this feeling operates like fireworks and lasts only for a few seconds? I have seen many people who come and tell me that they want to confess, they want to fast, they want to have Holy Communion, that they would do anything in order to get on the path of God, and in the end they do nothing! They do not fast, not even during Holy Week, and you remain wondering where all their enthusiasm went!

Our Christ is unique and wise. What wonderful words He chose in His parable to explain it all! The seeds that fell on the rocks withered, because they had no root («since they had no root»), that means that the passion of these people was superficial. It had no liveliness within; it had no freshness to help it grow («because it had no moisture»).

The second category of people that I mentioned to you based the change of their behaviour on an instant explosion, on an impulse which cooled off. It would have been much better if they had chosen to take things slowly, one thing at a time, every day, instead of doing a lot of things suddenly and then nothing, erasing everything.

When the Lord told the Apostles this parable, they asked Him to explain it to them. What is the path? What is the field where the seed sprouts immediately and withers after a little while? Or the one which grows and is choked by the thorns? And the Lord answered that the seeds that fall on the path symbolise the people who listen but then the devil comes and «takes away the word from their hearts that they may not believe and be saved». The devil does not let you listen, become holy, apply the truth. It is characteristic of the devil to make you forget, and not remember the things that you must remember. That means that a temptation comes and the devil does not want to let you think of Heaven, of God. He prods you to think of other things, he plays with your mind and you forget everything. Faith will lead you to salvation. When you believe that God exists, when you trust in God in your life, only then you are saved, because faith leads you to have experiences, to go through the struggles, to make the effort.

The Apostles then asked the Lord about the other seed, the one that grows on the rocks and withers after a little while. And the Lord answered that it was about the people who «when they hear the word, receive it with joy, but these have no root. They believe for a while and in time of temptation fall away». That means that they accept joyfully, with enthusiasm, like fireworks, what they hear, but they have no roots in order to keep it, apply it and make it happen.

Enthusiasm might lead a person to make decisions that many times will turn out for the best, but this is not the point. I remember once, in Sunday school, a boy who used to listen to Rock music and had a lot of cassette tapes (there were no CDs back then). So, I was explaining different things about this kind of music and at the end of Sunday school he asked me not to leave because he wanted to go home and bring me something. It made me wonder, but I waited for him to return. So, he comes back and he brings me a bag full of Rock music cassettes. «Take them, take all of them, I don't want them anymore, I don't want to have anything to do with this music. I understood how many things are hidden. How my soul becomes upset. I realised how satanic situations are sometimes hidden in this music. I want my soul to be clean. Take them». What had happened? His heart warmed up by the words he had heard, his soul blazed and he decided in that moment to begin the struggle. He asked me to throw away all the tapes, but I told him that I was not going to do that. «Look», I said to him, «I will take the cassettes, but I will not throw them away! Because, after a few days, you might change your mind about what you have done and Christ does not want you to be forced to change your life. I accept what you are doing! I am glad your soul has warmed up, but I want you to show this over a period of time. I want you to stay one month without the cassettes, two, three, five months and whenever temptation comes again, to be able to hold on and not listen. But, if you ever want them back, come and ask me for them. I will give them to you. Because the struggle that is worthy is the struggle that is voluntary, done willingly, and when you are in a position, consciously to choose between good and bad».

This boy needed to show if he had the roots to do that. Think, for example, of the flower pots we receive as gifts many times. In the beginning you see them beautiful, fully blossomed and after a little while they simply wither. This is because had not grown roots, in order to grow.

Enthusiasms are good, but they do not constitute a solid foundation for any decision. Someone, for example, gets enthusiastic about his life and wants to have a family. He finds a young woman and he thinks that she is the woman of his life and he immediately wants to marry her! No, this is not the way it should happen! This relationship needs time to grow roots. It needs to be tested through difficulties. You still have not even begun to know the other person. You have never quarrelled; there have been no misunderstandings yet in order for you to see how you would feel afterwards! When you go out, everything is fine. But wait, you need to find out the weaknesses of the other person. Then you will understand what happens and see if you still have that initial enthusiasm.

What I am saying about enthusiasm applies to all things, both human and divine. Because the person who deals with the human situations in a shallow and superficial way, in haste and enthusiasm, will do the same at the divine level also. Our life is a unified situation, the human and the divine elements are interconnected and interrelated. That is why the people who are virtuous and holy, are usually cautious when they see individuals being enthusiastic and on cloud nine. When they hear them say that they want to pray for hundreds of hours, to fast very strictly, when they exaggerate, they pull them back to slow them down a little.

This is because the sudden upbeats, unfortunately, are followed sometimes by sudden downfalls. This is why, my beloved, do not despair if you progress gradually, calmly, as much as you can, but steadily. If you can pray for five minutes a day, do that. Next year you may be able to pray for ten minutes, and after two years you might be able to pray for a quarter of an hour. Do as much as you can. And then you can become a person who loves prayer and if you choose to pray for many hours it will be a mature choice. But do not do many things hastily, because that is simply enthusiasm, it does not have depth or foundation.

Certainly, I do not want you to consider enthusiasm as something bad. You must also have joy in your life for what you are doing; you must enjoy it wholeheartedly. The point simply is to be able simultaneously to keep deepening. «But these have no root». We must not be like that, we must have root! We must be Christians who have been tried in life, who have gone through the challenges of life and remained with Christ, despite the trials. That is why the Lord said that they believe «for a while». For a little while, and then, as soon as they are faced with the first temptation, the first trial, they abandon everything.

A woman lost a child and since then she stopped going to church. When they asked her why she did that, she replied that, despite the fact that she used to go to church and pray regularly, made offerings, helped with the cleaning and more, God took her child away from her. She finished by saying «What kind of God is He? » God is not like we want Him to be, tailored to our needs and desires, Who promises us things that we would like. Yes, God promises us and gives us everything. He gives us Heaven, but we do not turn to Him for favours. We go to Him to mould us. We offer Him our soul, the field of our heart, and we ask for His help to make it fertile, to obtain a humble heart, so when He throws His Word we can be touched. This is the answer to the question I posed at the beginning: «Is it my fault for being the way I am? »

Christ gives you the answer. Initially, it is not your fault, but you are not a field without a soul. You are not land, you are not only soil. You also have a soul, which is immortal. You have logic, and above all, you have intention, inner desire. You may be light-hearted; you may be indifferent, cold, but within, you may want beauty and goodness even if you are not experiencing them. You may be saying to yourself: «Lord, I am not virtuous soil, my soul is not humble. I am harsh, stubborn, irritable, and disrespectful. I have many flaws. But I would love to …». This is intention.

«I would love, Lord, You, the farmer, You who can, change this field, because I cannot do it on my own. There is nothing growing within me, nor love, nor humility, nor charity, nor kindness. Nothing, only evil, unkindness and I have become harsh». Then Christ would answer you: «I am not scolding you for what you are. I am scolding you for what you are not becoming. And you can become, if you give me the possibility to enter your soul, enter your field and repair it. Do you want that? »

This is the difference between the parable and reality. The parable does not have absolute correlation with our soul, because our soul is not an idle field. It is not a deadened field like the soil of the earth. Our soul has reason, will and volition. The point is whether you are going to decide to make your desire real and ask the Lord to help you. I said at the beginning, the Lord does not scold, does not make negative comments, He simply and humbly describes. Christ says: «I did not come to judge the world but to save the world». When Christ comes to find you and you are in lethargy, bored with your life, bored and you do not want to go to church, you do not want to pray, He will not come to make remarks. He will simply ask you if you want to know Him better and let Him into your soul. He will not demand that you start immediately going to church, listening to the preaching, the lectures and all. This will happen eventually if your intention is good. The only thing that Christ awaits from you is your true desire, to show that you simply and really want, as long as you mean it.

At this point I would like us to pay special attention to something. Never tell God anything that you do not take seriously! Christ treats you with seriousness not shallowness. When you speak with Him, he listens to you very seriously and He gives you His whole heart. He turns His ear to listen to you and whatever you ask Him, He will give it to you, at the corresponding cost and procedure that you need to go through in order to receive it. So, what does that mean? When you ask the Lord to relieve you of your flaws, to change your soul and make you a new person, Christ starts working, He begins correcting you, to make your field fertile and fruitful. In order for that to happen, it needs digging with the plough, the coulter, which goes deep into the field, turning over the soil and breaking the stones. This means that it needs pressure that will bring about pain and tears. So, when you ask the Lord to change your life and make you humble, it means that you are ready to begin that procedure.

So, God comes and tells you that the field of your soul will soften with pain. Once you have asked God for help, you accept all that He will bring your way. If you lose your job, God will reply that this happened because He was fulfilling your prayer. «But God, I did not pray to lose my job ...», you will say. «Yes, my child, but you were asking to soften the soil of your soul. This job you lost softened you a little. Do you remember? You were humbled». «Yes, but the other day at work I was treated very badly..., and the time when my wife got ill..., and the other time when I had that accident..., and then when...? » God will reply: «All these things are the dialogue I am having with you! » «But Lord, you are being very hard on me! »

«I am not the one who is hard on you. It is your soul which is very harsh and when I try to touch it, you get this feeling of hardship as if it is coming from Me, but it exists within you. It cannot be done otherwise! The soul you are carrying will soften and be humbled only after it has gone through a lot of pain». «That much? Taking my child away from me? » (as that woman I mentioned to you earlier was saying). And the Lord does not answer, he only reaches out His hands upon Golgotha and shows us His cross, how He holds His cross. And he says to us: «Here is the answer».

It cannot be done otherwise. It is the only way for the field of our heart to soften. That is why I tell you that God takes very seriously what we ask Him. He does not toy with us, He wants to save us. The quicker our soul is humbled, the quicker it will be corrected and softened. Then there will be no reason for us to suffer any more. Unless God wants to make us Saints so we can shine like the sun. But we, my brothers and sisters, do not belong in that category. Christ is still breaking the big pieces of our ego that have become huge rocks inside our hearts.

Another similar challenge is cancer. Father Paisios (pronounced pa – ee – sios) says that on Mount Athos he met an elder, who held quite a high position in the monastery. This elder was a very harsh and selfish person, with a very authoritarian attitude who looked down on others. You never dared tell him anything, and he never asked for anything in a kind way, he only demanded. At one time, the elder got cancer and Father Paisios stood by his side helping him with everything he needed. The Father told me that cancer had completely transformed this man's soul, it taught him humility and he became gentle and kind-hearted with other people. Father Paisios wondered at how the illness had transformed him. It seems that the elder had good intention within − besides, for him to go to Mount Athos and devote his life to God, there must have been something good hidden within him, no matter how strange he was. Obviously, it was upon that something good, that God based the transformation of this person's soul into a fertile humble field. He decided to sow into him virtues: love, humility, kindness, gentleness of the soul, gratitude, and He achieved that with the blows, the digging and ploughing, tears and pain. The individuals who have suffered are the ones who help and teach. They teach all of us to soften, to be humble, to awaken, and to get out of the lethargy we are living and understand the futility of this life and the seriousness of our salvation. To awaken in order to save our souls!

One day, a twenty-five-year-old man said to me: «The point is to not lose my soul! I want to save my soul. I do not care how or when. Whether I am here, become a monk, go to Mount Athos, marry or become a missionary. The only thing I am interested in is how to save my soul, through any path. » And yet, we drown in the futilities of life and we forget this major issue and life slips through our hands. Our own life robs us.

Besides, this is what the Lord says when He refers to the other category, the seed which falls among the thorns. «And the thorns grew with it and choked it», that means, the seed grows, the plant begins to grow, but close by the thorns and the other weeds choke it and it cannot grow. And the Lord goes on: «And as for what fell among the thorns, they are those who hear, but as go on their way they are choked by the cares and riches and pleasures of life, and their fruit does not mature». These people cannot cultivate their soul because they are preoccupied and drowned in their concerns, riches and pleasures of life. Today there are thousands of things on our minds and we do not have the time to tend to our soul.

One time I was having a discussion with someone and I was telling him about the end of time events that await us and about the Second Coming. He said to me: «What are you talking about? I have to finish my dissertation; I have to get my Master's degree! What Second Coming are you talking about? The Second Coming cannot happen now! I still have so many things to do. It cannot happen now!» I know that sounds funny, but that is the way it is. You may not have to finish a dissertation, but if you take a look at your life, if you realise how many things you are preoccupied with, you will understand that in your own way you have also forgotten the central theme of your life, which is Christ and your meeting with Him.

Are you ready? If God tells you today that He wants to meet you, if He tells you to leave everything you have been doing to go to Him? I am certain that you will tell Him that you cannot, because you have a family, property, things to do, obligations! But these things will never cease! God gave you all these things in order to lead you to Him. Essentially, all these things constitute a kind of help, so that you can approach Him. And do you know what has happened to you? You have been absorbed by all these things, you live on earth and you are growing roots. You are stuck, you are standing still. Our Christ asks us to get unstuck from this earth, not to get drowned in the mundane things, because all the things we have to do, from the simpler ones, such as cooking or doing the shopping, to the more complex ones, such as our studies, professional goals etc. are never going to end. Our heart does not want to be absorbed by all these things, because they are unsubstantial. Think of your grandparents, think of your great grandparents, where are they? Are they still alive? Think where they are right now, despite the fact that they too built, cooked, had a family, had dreams that they wanted to fulfil. Where are they now? They are in a small box.... Did all these dreams fit into a little box? No. In the end what is left of a human being are just a few bones. However, these few bones cannot be satisfied with all the earth and all its goods and riches. Why? Because God has created us in a way not to be satisfied with anything in this world so we will thirst for Heaven, for the absolute, the perfect and infinite which is God. So, we would not fall into this trap and choke.

Tonight think of what you are going to do the next day from first thing in the morning till late at night or what you did yesterday all day and contemplate, which of all the things that you did you will need the day you meet Christ, essentially, the day you save your soul and what will be left from your flesh will be a few bones. I am not telling you this to frighten you; I am telling you this to help you understand the truth! You must get ready, not to die, but to live! But in order to live, you must learn the secrets of life. I am for life, for eternal life and Resurrection. I am not for death, and I do not want my words to smell death, but life. But in order to understand life, you must understand the deception of this world so it does not captivate you.

This is what the whole world is all about. A deception, it makes fun of us, it robs us, it makes us forget what is essential, permanent, infinite, even God Himself, and in the end we wonder: «But, where did everything go?» In life, concerns, chores, riches and pleasures are not everything. There are many people who would love to pray, but cannot find the time, because they are very busy. It is not that you are a bad person and you do not want to pray. You would love to, but you say that you do not have the time, because, for example, you have to do the ironing, then you have to go to do the shopping, then you need to come back and put away your groceries and provisions, cook, put the children to sleep and so on. In the end, the whole day passes without you realising it and you have done nothing! What is the secret? Include prayer in everything you do. Do not stop doing the things you have to do, but do not let them absorb you; do not let them rob you.

Speaking about the field, and sowing seeds as a farmer, the Lord gave you reason and nourishment for thought and deepening. He found the depth of being, the reason for being, as the Holy Fathers say, which means that He looks around and the world does not frighten Him, nor does He consider the world as something bad that we must deny. We simply must not get stuck. Besides, we have previously mentioned that the material things exist in order to help us go closer to God. Christ, however, sees earth but he does not stay at that. He tells you to look at how the seed falls on the ground and tend to your soul accordingly. He looks at the birds and sees more than birds flying. He says that little birds fly without worry because they are taken care of by our heavenly Father; you must trust God in the same way. He sees the beautiful flowers and He explains that they are so beautiful because they are not anxious and He encourages you to release anxiety from your life so you can become equally beautiful. Your soul, your body and your face will become beautiful, you will find serenity. This is the secret. Live in the world, within the chores that you cannot avoid, in the riches and the pleasures that God gives you, like food, drink, family, love, but above all tend to your soul. He has not given us all these things with bad intention, nor has He given us these things in order to scold us for using them. He has given us these things so we can enjoy them with an appreciative intention, not to drown in them and overuse them. That is the difference.

God gave us food, to be thankful and happy that we have eaten, and grateful to Him for our luck. He has given us food so we can think of our fellow humans who have nothing to eat and help them. He has given us all the beautiful things so we can look at them also in a way that leads us to deeper and higher levels, as Christ sees nature, using parables, as He sees the material world and talks about the divine. He sees the barren fig tree and talks about the infertility and hypocrisy of the synagogue. He looks at the celestial phenomena and He understands if the weather is going to be cold or hot, and in the same way He encourages us to learn to perceive the signs of the times. Whatever He sees around Him constitutes a reason to teach us to soften our soul and feel God in everything there is around us. There was a Holy man who would look at the sunset and say: «Just like the sun sets today, my life will also set one day. The sunset will come.» He would look at the sunrise and say: «Lord, just as the sun is rising, may the sun of Your love rise in my heart.» He would wash his face and say: «Lord, just as I am washing my face with water, may I cleanse my soul and my inner self.» He would look at the rain falling and say: «Lord, just as the drops of rain are falling, may tears fall from my eyes, out of love for the world, for the pain of the world, out of love for You, to soften my soul.» He would look at a dried branch and say: «Lord, this is how my soul is. It has dried out because of my selfishness.»

We must learn to use the concerns, riches and pleasures as God wants. Not to deny them, but to use them as means to transcend them, rise above them and see God's grace, His love. See the face of Christ who is seeking us out through all these things. Otherwise, we will drown in God's gifts, in our achievements and we will be destroyed in our own happiness. Doesn't this sound crazy and oxymoron? It is true and, unfortunately, we are living it. We are experiencing a terrible cultural explosion, technological, electronic, and internet-wise. An explosion of offers, unique potentials in our times, and yet our planet, our lives, the salvation of our world as well as that of our souls are in danger. And all this in an era when we have everything!

When you quarrel with your wife and go out on the balcony to smoke a cigarette, there may be a rose bush. But, while you are smoking, you are irritated and you can see nothing else. You cannot see the rose which is blossoming; you cannot smell the aroma which is piercing your nose. Nothing touches you. You are living in your own world, in your selfishness, in your hardened heart. God gives us infinite possibilities to soften our souls, to make it a good and virtuous land, but we do not get the messages, because we are living within our passions. And the worst of all is that we do not want to get out of them…. We all have passions and weaknesses, but what is tragic, is not wanting to get out. The best thing you and I and all of us can do is pray to the Lord to make our soul a humble land, a virtuous land, a fertile land, so that it can absorb what the Lord gives us, especially His love, which we turn away from every day. Know that it hurts. If you ask for it, be prepared to suffer, to bleed. But it is worth it, because in the end you will be saved. What do you prefer? To be one hundred years old and have a soul which is barren and unfertile, or to soften your heart and let God take you any way He chooses?

It goes without saying that we are going to be asking the Lord: «Lead us not into temptation». We are human beings; we cannot endure many blows, the suffering and the tears. Only the Saints asked to give themselves to God and said: «Lord, I did whatever you wanted. Give me whatever You want, even cancer. Just save me».

My brothers and sisters, my wish is that we will not resist God's love which comes to turn our souls into good and virtuous soil that, with patience will become fruitful.

This is the only salvation…

ALONE AT CHRISTMAS

Translation: Giorgos Migadakis

"I have been listening to your broadcasts for a long time,
but last night you spoke to my heart. I live alone;
I was feeling loneliness very intensely.
I am an immigrant in Germany..."
T.P. Germany (e-mail)

What a happy day this is, dear listeners of the church of Piraeus. Greetings, I wish you a merry Christmas! It's already Christmas time, we reached Christmas, we sense Christmas, we enjoy these days. Since yesterday! And it is a very festive atmosphere. You are all very happy; aren't you? I can imagine...You are having a lovely time, with your families, preparing to go out to eat, to enjoy, to have fun, to wish Merry Christmas to other people. To buy gifts and candies from the pastry, to visit your loved ones and gain some extra weight, so that you can forget about diets, the effort of fasting, or whatever problem everyone has. So that we can start to feel pleasure, isn't like that? Isn't it so?! Somebody tells me that is not so.

Somebody tells me: "Father, it is not just you in the world, it is not just you, who feels the joy of Christmas"- I answer, "Oh, I have to finish the radio show quickly because I have dinner plans, I had many invitations for today, and I didn't know which one to choose." But somebody is talking to me again...and says... "Father, could you stop talking, for a moment, about all of you, who feel happy today, this joyful and festive day?" "And who shall I talk about?" I responded.

"You should talk about the sadness of these days, because we exist, too". "Who are you, the ones who say that you exist?" "The ones", he says, "who are not in a car right now, the ones who won't go and visit someone, the ones who will listen to the Church of Piraeus radio station at noon, while you have turned off your radio because you will be eating, drinking, listening to music, having fun and watching films on TV. We cannot follow your schedule, the one that you - the celebrating people- have." "And who are you?" "Father" he says "say something about the sadness of these festive days. Speak about us for a moment; we also exist in this world. We exist and we listen to the Church of Piraeus radio station and we will continue–even if it is Christmas–to be inside our loneliness, our silence, hurting." Look, let's specify something; let's specify. If I'm planning to do a radio show like this, and I'm obliged to do it, I'll do it. But sometimes, I'm just saying, that maybe you, the one who tells me that you are not invited to have dinner somewhere today, are also responsible for that the loneliness. Maybe it is also your fault that you are not invited to join a lovely, friendly dinner. Maybe it's because of you: maybe this loneliness exists because you made this choice. Because I know that some people get invited· some people are loved and people want to be around them, but due to the fact that you have low self-esteem, a low acceptance of yourself, you have –to put it differently– a secret ego, you are stubborn and you don't want to go. And then you are sitting alone, being upset and later on, you are also feeling blue.

"I'm not wanted by anyone" the voice says. When you are invited to go somewhere you do not go. When you sit all alone you become upset. Perhaps it is your fault? Maybe you are responsible that you are alone today. I don't know for sure, we are discussing it now, at the Church of Piraeus this day. I don't know how many people are listening right now, because I know that most of them are in a hurry to prepare for tonight. To leave their houses, and go out to have fun, to enjoy themselves. But I'm thinking that maybe the people who sit all alone can still make it and go out as well. It's a few minutes past one, you can still make it! You can make a phone call and say that, actually, you will go out! You will say, "I'll come, I'll also come to the dinner that you invited me." Do it, don't stay alone today, if there's no serious reason, if it's not your choice. Because it's a different matter, the v o l u n t a r y loneliness of a monk, an ascetic, a man who lives alone because he feels the fullness of Christ's presence and because this is the choice he made in life. Because that's not loneliness, when you feel Christ by your side this day, when you feel large peace, immense happiness, endless surfeit. Even before you eat you feel full in your soul, full of happiness. So that's why this is not loneliness. For example, Father Paisios, if he were alive today, he would have gone to the nearby monastery to be present at the Divine Liturgy, then to receive Holy Communion, to eat with other monks and return to his little cell, being very happy. All alone but happy. Because he feels full. He is not just alone but all alone, away from people, but full from the presence of Christ. If you are experiencing something like this, then ok. You are doing the right thing by being alone.

But maybe we are also responsible for being alone on such a day? Maybe we are sometimes a bit odd? A little fussy and unusual? I don't know, I'm just asking. Maybe someone is not responsible at all about all these things, maybe someone's behaviour is a bit strange, he is unsociable and he's responsible for not making the first step or not responding. Maybe sometimes your behaviour bothers other people and they are having a hard time with you. Look: Even if it is like that, don't be disappointed. Because, if you are disappointed, it conceals ego. If you are responsible in all these things, make them all material for humility. Say: This year I'm beginning to understand myself a little. I am a bit odd. Nobody invited me, nobody wants me. Maybe it's my fault and I'm not very friendly, very sociable, very hearty, very beloved with my ego. Admit it. Admit who you are. Admit that sometimes you are an abrasive character. And you know, if you admit it, Christ will love you: He will love you, because it will be like saying to Him, "Lord, this year that you were born again, I'm in need, in need of Your birth, I will give You work, I will give You work to do on my soul, Lord. I am a strange person, come and fix me. Come and heal me. I'm also a troubled man. There, Lord, you were born and no one called me to go out to dinner. No one wants me; no one wants to see me. I am the one to blame—maybe sometimes I am the one to blame."

So, you, who are responsible, the ones who are responsible, we are all responsible to an extent that we are not the people we are supposed to be. Let's do our self-criticism. Let's be humble, let's repent and ask from God mercy and beg Him, from now on. I know that there are others of you who listen right now, and you are waiting and saying to yourselves: "When is it going to be my turn at the 'Unseen Crossings,' will the speaker mention a little something about us? Because we are not the ones to blame. You are doing the right thing to say that a man is responsible for not being invited to the Christmas dinner; but why is it my fault?"

"It's not my fault; I ..." Now I'll speak about you... "I am sick," you will say. "I am sick, I am in the hospital. And now I have a small radio and I listen to you, next to my commode. And you, father, started shouting saying that it's our fault, that we are selfish and you said..." No, I'm not talking about you. Now it is indeed not your fault. You are sick, helpless, you are in pain, and you can't go anywhere. And everybody loves you, but necessarily you live alone. They will come to visit you, someone will come to see you, some came in the morning, but now they left for lunch. Someone is physically helpless, Yes, and someone is paralyzed, I know that you are paralyzed. What can you do about it? Is it your fault that it happened to you? That you can't run, you can't go and show what your heart feels? Your heart wants to run, but your body doesn't help you. And it's Christmas...Yes, it's not your fault and it's not your fault that you live alone, because you have no relatives. You are a lonely person, because you don't have relatives. Because you are an old man, you are an old person. You are an old woman, a grandfather, a grandmother.

Yes, I know...Now you are crying; now you are crying because you have a heavy grief, and this year you cannot do the things you did, because you feel great pain. Someone isn't home this year. Yes, it's horrible. This is also horrible. So, if you want, I will keep you company.

To talk a little about these people who today, Christmas day, who cannot, although it's not their fault, under the circumstances they stay alone. They stay alone without much company, just a few people or no one next to them. And they are lonely people, and they are sad and then a wave of melancholy comes. First of all let me tell you something comforting about you. Everyone feels a bit blue during the holidays. And it's not happiness 100 % all day and all night. There are some moments that the wave of melancholy finds us even in the happiest moments of our lives. A sorrow comes, the psychologists and sociologists say, the sorrow of the holiday seasons. The sorrow of Easter, the sorrow of Christmas. It really affects us for a bit. Our soul is grieving; we cannot fit the joy, the absolute joy. And as humans on this planet, our joy is combined with sorrow. We are going to be happy and also sad. You see someone will get married and some people will be sad, because their child is going away. Now are you happy or sad? Both: I feel sad and happy. I'm feeling blue and happy. Everyone feels that from time to time.

So, it's not only you. Don't exaggerate things. Don't feel miserable and jealous because the rest of the world is happy. "Today, Christmas, I feel," you say, "like the crummiest." It's not like that. Make good thoughts. Father Paisios puts it in a beautiful way: "Make good thoughts, think positive things. Like God wants them. See things with positivity." Like they say: If you see the glass with water until the middle, say that it is half-full, don't say half-empty, say that it is half-full: it is not a lie! It is half-full and also half-empty. Buy you should not look on empty things. See the glass full. See the positive side of things and say: I'm in a free country. I'm Christian orthodox. I'm able to hear the church of Piraeus. I can pray. Think of something good you have. Something little, something little you can do. Remember a child who told me: "I'm disabled; I'm paralysed all over my body· but for some time now I can move my head; the rest of the body stays motionless. I can move my head and I'm happy. Look! You see something positive in your sorrow. Don't be miserable. Melancholy will lead you even lower. No, look at it in a positive way. Search to find something positive. "I don't find anything," you say. That's also positive, the fact that you don't have anything and you rely on God!

Make this positive thought. Say: "Lord, I will rely on you. Only you. I don't have anything positive. There is nothing good in my life. I don't find anything pleasant to say about myself." Surely there is something good. View it by faith. God wants to lead you somewhere with this loneliness. He wants to lead you somewhere. He is God, right? Isn't He wise? Doesn't He love you? Doesn't He control when the sun comes out and when it leaves? Doesn't He control the birds that fly in the sky, the leaves that fall, how many hairs we have on our head? Doesn't He know everything? So? Our Christ knew that this year at Christmas you, or he or she, (you are not alone), will live this Christmas like this: lonely. With a lonely way. See that also in God's love, that is what God wanted, God knew, God allows. God signed this day and said: "you my child with the wisdom that I have and the omniscience and the love I have, I know everything for you, and I judge that this is the way you have to spend this day. I allow it...I allow it."

It doesn't mean that God is happy with the way you live· but He allows it for a good cause. View it by faith, view it with faith in Christ: "And we know that all things work together for good to those who love God and to those who are called according to his purpose." Do you love God? This loneliness will lead you somewhere good. This sorrow will lead you somewhere good. And this tear, it will lead you somewhere good. So, view it by faith, this thing you are going through today, and try to see it in a way that will benefit you. It will lead to something good. You will pull from the bitterness of it... something good will come. From the bitterness you will put something sweet in your soul. Today you can– if you want– be connected, be connected with Christ· to wear His shoes: to enter also – if you want– in the loneliness of Christ. He was also alone in this world, when he was born. People didn't accept Him with joy. He lived a lonely life. The birth of Christ–unlike today with mangers we make and the beautiful ornaments in the streets, with the little kids and Santa Claus – when Christ was born, He came in a lonely way to the world. The Virgin Mary kept Him warm with Her love, with Her arms, with Her warm kisses. Yes, indeed the angels praised Him and some shepherds; but after that he was left alone. Most people didn't pay attention to Him. So just think that today you see things through the life of Christ. You are being humiliated for a bit, just like Christ. Today you are alone, just like Christ was. And you can—if you want— be connected, be connected a little bit more with Him and say: "Lord, please show understanding to me...Show understanding, You, who waited for love and didn't receive it. Just like that, I was waiting for some love today and I didn't receive love and I am alone." And you can connect yourself with Christ in His own measure of loneliness, humiliation, reduction and marginalization. Are you in the margin? You are in the margin, just like Christ was today. And we are to be crucified—isn't that what we say on Easter? – with Christ.

So today I look like Christ, I who love Christ so much. Only those who are alone just like Him, those who are in the margin just like Him, look like Christ! Be patient. We will learn the word "patience." This day will pass and so will the rest of our days. The other days of our lives will also pass. Our entire life will pass and it will be one day. This life is going to pass too. God will find something good in your heart from this loneliness. And try to feel a little, if you want....Because it's a different thing to talk to afflicted people, lonely people if you are yourself a lonely person. Giving advice is so easy, but the person who is in pain cannot stand it. It's different when you are in pain and people come to give you a lesson. It's not something we like. So I'm not being a teacher here. I'm just saying what I remember from Saint Isaac of Syria when he said: "Try to feel who is on earth, you and your God. Try to rest in your heart not in a selfish way. Try not to pay attention, if other people exist and if you don't need others; but feel that God loves you like you are alone in the world!" He loves you just like if you were alone on earth. Live your life just you and God, not in a selfish way, but personal, that God loves you personally. That He comes to you, He doesn't just go to other people's living rooms, to the parties, family visits, leaving you aside... "Wait, I have other things to do now and..." No! He loves you as if you were the only one born in this world. The newborn Christ was going to come to earth even for that one person, he says. What a huge love that is!

No one calls you? I think after the show is over, the ones who listen will make some calls. Your friends will also call you, from the church of Piraeus, your spiritual brothers. But even if no one calls you, know that in this day Christ loves you. And that He is devoted to you exclusively. Feel your personal God. Even if no one existed on earth, you were going to be born, Lord, just for me, and you want to make Christmas just for my soul! And that is very beautiful! It will help you live in a mental integrity without feeling pathologically dependent –in the matter of joy– from other people. "Lord I know you love me, you are my God. And while You are being shared with all of us, you are devoted to each person personally, with infinite fullness. And I want to feel you that way." You and God on earth! Just you and God! This fact shall fill you with joy! And then you will see the others with kindness, and you will be happy with their happiness. You won't be jealous. Don't be jealous, don't envy. You won't dislike, you won't hate others–like some people, who because they see other people happy they want to take revenge on them. Jealousy becomes rage. They become angry and upset, and dislike people who feel happy. Because they say: Everyone is happy and I am sad. No! you'll say. I have my God; I have my Christ that was His will. He loves me also and I can stand it!

Let me tell you something else. It is possible, until tonight, that you will also live a miracle! You never know what happens. Maybe something will happen to your soul, maybe a joy will come to your life, maybe you will hear or see something, and maybe something will happen that will make you feel happy. Don't allow this melancholy to expand. Live with this hope, don't allow hope to die in your soul. Wait a little. The rest of you, who listen and feel fine and have nothing of the things we discuss, pray for those who have these things. While you are not paying attention, because in a minute you will be parking your car and entering your friend's house to celebrate. You will get out of the car, close the radio and start having fun while we will continue the show. We will continue with those who are in pain. With those who are lonely. With those without company for tonight. And because of that, let the prayer, the love be with us, with each other, in order to feel in our hearts that we are not lonely people, we who will continue.

You know something else : our life is tinted with sorrow. Even the biggest joy hides a bit of sadness. I said this at the beginning. When Kazantzakis went once to Mount Athos, he went to a monastery; I think it was the monastery of St. Dionysius, which is rather small. He saw, he said, a bush outside. They say that on the leaves of that bush you saw little images of the crucified Christ and the sorrow of the cross. And Kazantzakis said to a monk: "Your monastery is very narrow, you feel bad in here. It is so narrow." And the monk said: "It's not the monastery responsible for the narrowness you feel. It's the world that is narrow: the world cannot stand us, time cannot stand us! And the space of this planet, of this earth, of this life. We cannot fit, that's why we feel sad. We want the absolute, the endless. We ask for much and we cannot fit in that. We cannot."

There is a sorrow coloring our lives, a loneliness, even in the presence of many people. I remember, when I was a kid, I had an art teacher. She was once determined to organize in the area we live an exhibition with earthen structures, painting and crafts; we were in high school, and she managed to do it. Many people came: the mayor, the bishop. They said a blessing, and later they put on some music and did the opening of the exhibition. And I was happy. So, well, how happy was our teacher that her dream came true? I reached her in the crowd, with a lot of people around us, and everyone was greeting her... "Congratulations!!" they said to her, and so on. I said to her: "Mrs. –I was in second grade– "I imagine that you are very happy! Come on! Your wish became a reality"! And she told me: "Haven't you heard that in the crowd you can feel all alone?" I was left speechless. "Excuse me, is this how you feel?" And she said: "If I say that it is like that, it is like that." Then someone came to greet her and I left and she didn't give me any notice. And it's been– how many? – twenty years and I still remember what she said to me: "Feeling lonely inside a crowd." During the Christmas dinner someone might feel a wave of loneliness. This life is mixed with relativity. The most beautiful thing is tinged with pain, bitterness, with a gap.

Something shows up to remind us that we are still on earth, to remind us that we are still...low. That we are not close to God, close to absolute happiness. There is: "a place where there is no pain, sorrow or grieving, a place of green pasture, in a place of refreshment, from whence pain, sorrow and mourning have fled away."...what are these things? "A place of refreshment, from whence pain, sorrow and mourning have fled away." There is mourning here. Mourning will come in a little bit. It will start with your mother's mourning, when she tidies up the house. Happiness and sorrow are together in this life. So, remember this: the monastery isn't narrow, the atmosphere you live is not narrow and you think that you are upset. It's the whole world. Our planet is narrow. And absolute happiness does not exist in this world.

Such is life. And also you should know this. You who feel lonely can teach the others. You teach. You teach right now with your patience. You teach others to be humble, to be strong, and to be grateful with nothing. Some people know that you are alone— they do. Do you think they are not concerned? Do you know what they say inside them? "Think of this woman, just think of this person. How can she stand it? How can he stand the sorrow, the pain, the disability, the paralysis, the grief, the illness or any unhappiness? She is alone." They say this. You teach and become a preacher. You teach with your example, when this example is to live humbly and to admit the truth, without reacting. Because if you react, then you don't teach. But when you are not reacting, it is very beautiful.

Anyway, I don't have knowledge of everyone's situation. But whatever happens, be humble. The solution, the Saints say, for every sadness we have, every loneliness, every contempt, is humiliation. So learn to consider yourself unworthy for the big gifts. Say to yourself inside you: "It's ok, Lord; I'm insignificant. I'm small. The happiness, the joy I want, it's not for me, I don't deserve it." One cannot say: "I demand to be happy. I demand that people will call me. You are all horrible people, you are all bad. No one loves me. I demand it." You cannot demand, you cannot demand. Feel insignificant and say to yourself inside you —not disadvantaged, but humble... — "Lord you are doing the right thing, with the way you are treating me! I deserve it, this is what I deserve: to be alone. Ok, if You wanted You would have given it to me, I cannot stubbornly demand it. You will give it to me, this time You think it's right, whatever You want. I cannot demand. I can beg! Begging is a different thing from demanding. I beg, I am a beggar." I say: "Lord, as You want. It's not my right. Blessed art Thou, O Lord, teach me Thy statutes. It's your right to do what You want." I cannot say: I have the right to be happy, the right to happiness. It's not a right. It's a gift that God gives if He wants. And the example of that is what we live today. God chose for you today to live in loneliness.

God allows it for something good. If you see it with gratitude and humiliation, do you know how much it will benefit you? Very much. You will be a Saint today. A halo will be placed on your head. A halo! You will shine! A monk said, that one time when they served food, they served the others first and there wasn't enough food for him. They didn't have a plate with food for him. And he didn't say anything. Do you know what he says inside him? He said that the first wave was to demand. What is going on...I'm not going to stand for it. Wait a minute...Don't I have the right to eat? I want to have my food too, bring me food. Then he thought not to say anything. Lord, so many days that I ate was a gift. I realised it just now. You were giving me food. I cannot demand. And do you know what I'm going to do? I will pray: "Christ our God, bless the food and the drink of your servants"... Everyone ate. He sat, waited and drinking his water, then he stood up, as they thanked the Lord, and he didn't consider himself worthy of eating. He didn't ask to eat. He didn't demand it. He was humiliated. He found a reason to be humiliated. If you do this, you won't be demanding. And if you don't ask, He will give you everything. The One who came is everything! Christ is everything. If you humiliate yourself, He will come to you. He who is everything. And if everything comes, your soul will be filled and maybe your body, without a lot of food, but with a lot of grace, a lot of love and a lot of truth from Christ!

And let me tell you something else. Now that we consoled a little and we brought out our pain and we talked about your sadness, we let it out. A child tells me: "My grandmother, when she hears you on the radio, she cries. Between one and two o'clock in the afternoon, she cries." "She cries?" I said. "Why is she crying? I am not saying something to cry about".... " Uh...she sits down and thinks about what you say and feels some of them." So, now we said some of our own, we let it out. The lonely ones.

Now do you want to do something else? Shall we do a counterattack? A love counterattack! The lonely of this world, the lonely of the church of Piraeus, the ones who are listening to the show right now and who are alone for some reason, let's unite and make a love attack. A counterattack. And say: Today is Christmas! Today is such a nice day, you are having fun, and you feel happy, Congratulations! Enjoy yourselves! We are not jealous of you, we don't hate you, and we don't feel envy. We will, however, make our own visits. The lonely ones–you, and you the paralysed, and you the monk, the nun, the ones who listen to the show, even if you are in your little cell and even if you are sick at the hospital–we will make a visit!...How? We will make a visit with our prayer and love. When you love and pray for the others, even if you are hidden in some cave on earth, the atmosphere fills with waves: waves of grace, waves of Divine mercy. This is something that travels and can go anywhere. Maybe now that you are here, wherever you are, in Athens, in Patra, in Aigio, in Kalamata, wherever you can hear the church of Piraeus. Right now people are calling and saying: we listen through the internet to the church of Piraeus and we are happy. I have calls fron Brussells, from France, from

America. We listen to you! So, if the radio station of the church of Piraeus – which is a technical instrument – can reach so far, think about the prayer! You can pray right now and send a wave, an ocean of love, to America, to Germany, to Australia, to the North pole, to the Missionary, to the North Epirus who are Missionaries, wherever you want!...So come and unite and send big waves. Let's join our forces and make a prayer. Let's do some visits. The lonely people, the ones who are alone, make visits. So, make a visit, if you want, to Nursing Homes. Let's go to the Nursing Homes, to the rooms! And you, the one who listens now and you are in a nursing home, make your own visit. Where? To the nearby rooms, to the next floor, where there are also other people. You sit alone and look at the pictures of your children, you are sad, you are crying. You say, I'm alone. Come on, you are not alone! There are others! Think about the others, they have problems also and they are alone. And they have no company whatsoever. Think about those in pain. You are not the only one with a painful and bloody heart. There are many others. Make a visit everywhere in the planet to the lonely people who have no one. They have no one. Right? You have at least someone.

Let me tell you something, not in a selfish way: you also have the Church of Piraeus: You can hear now a few words, we are talking to you. I'm keeping you company. The others, however, they have no one. And when we say no one, we mean no one! And they turn on the radio to listen to beautiful songs, the news, what is going on in the countries of the world. They were expecting Christmas. Yes, but this isn't comfort, it's not a strong comfort. The heart remains untouched. There are people today who reach the limits of madness because of the loneliness and the unbelievable melancholy they feel. They take medicines in order to calm down. Their soul cannot rest. And you know: you have

Christ! The most important thing: you have faith! You believe. You are alone but you believe in God. You won't be mad. You have God. Like someone once said: Without God, I would have gone crazy. This isn't a small thing. To have Christ giving you strength. To be alone with Christ. It's a very big deal indeed.

So, make a visit. Make a visit and imagine. And go and say a simple "Hello." "Hello, I came to give you a kiss, to give a soft touch, to tell you "Christ is born." Christ is born, take courage. Christ is here to give us strength, to give us hope. We don't speak about illusions, about fairytales, that everything is beautiful and pleasant. But He came, the One who will give us strength to make everything pleasant." And go make a mental visit. Now leave the nursing homes and those people and go to the benches, to the benches in the squares. Go to the halls of the stations. Go to the alleys of the cities. Go to the dirty rooms where there are −right now as we are speaking− the drug addicts.

Go there and say "Hello" with your prayer. Pray a little for them. You should see how much they suffer today! How perfectly unhappy they are. Addicted to substances. They tear up their soul and their body. And give some love to those people. Pray a little for these drug addicts. They are spending Christmas away from their families, because their families sometimes cannot even find them, because they disappear. They cannot have them at the Christmas table either, because they won't go, and they can't feel happy. They don't understand: they just take drugs and live in their personal world, an imaginary and fake world. A world of deception and destruction. In the land of the white death. And they are in so much suffering. Make a visit to them. They are also alone and they can't pray; at least you can pray "Lord show mercy" to them. You can. An acquaintance of mine once told me–her son was having a drug problem– that she entered his room and saw him with his own hand floating in the air holding a shoe with the lace hanging. And he was waiting, she said, to tie the lace, but at that moment he went under the influence of the drug. He was as still as a stone. He had a cold stare, with the shoe hanging by the lace, and she was speaking to him, but her son couldn't understand.

So, go to that person who is still as a stone, to that child who has experienced this situation of blur, in the soul and the body, and make a little prayer, hug him, and take your rosary and say: "Lord, Jesus Christ, show mercy on your servants, to the people who suffer, who are drug addicts. Today is Christmas, the biggest joy, the most sweet consolation, but they can't be comforted, My Christ. Instead of You, instead they use drugs. Even today they use drugs." Make a visit, do you know how far can you go? You, the ones who stay still, the lonely ones of this day, just with your prayer...I know...I know... I've made you feel a bit stuffy. Get out a little, get out of the rooms of the drug addicts. Get out and let's go somewhere farther, let's go to the highway, to the large roads of the world. Let's go there where there is more air, and cool ourselves. Make a visit there.

And make a prayer for those who are driving right now: thousands of cars, millions of cars. They are being driven at this moment on the entire planet Earth. Some go to have fun, some go to work, others are working and going and in a little bit, they are driving to go, and they will eat well. And please pray for them to return safely, not drunk, make a prayer to return alive and not dead. Pray for them to be well while they are driving so there will be no accidents, no injuries, on their way home. If five of them went out to make a visit, let's pray for all of them to come back. Not half of them, some of them inside a hospital and the others dead, having their blood left on the road. Pray for those who are driving. Father Paisios, an isolated monk, but not a lonely person, had the earth filled with angels, he had filled the earth with the grace of God. He lit, he says, some cans and put candles in them, even when he was asleep and left the candle to burn saying: "Lord, this candle is for the sick, for the drug addicts, this for the good health of someone" and he was praying for all of them. And he made visits to Mount Athos. He went out few times, but he went out more than any of us did. He had travelled all over earth. He had visited all the places through his prayers, he had become, like he said, an astronaut of the sky. Having a vehicle...and for fuel a little cracker. He ate a cracker and made a long journey with that cracker. He was embracing the entire earth with his prayer. And he was praying with love for the entire world.

Do that yourself: become an astronaut of God. Get out of the attraction of earth, this gravitational force and enter the love of God. And embrace, pray for everybody, and then get out. Let's go again for a bit to the highway, to enter the small road, inside the city and go to the hospitals, to the Emergency Room, let's go where the sign says: "No entrance," we will get in! So we enter there, where the big surgeries are, the ones that last 8 to 15 hours, where the incubated people are, with oxygen masks, with serum...and they see their heart beat, full of cords. Here the people cannot breathe, they don't know how many hours they are going to live. There their angel is coming close to them and he doesn't know if finally, this soul will leave the body, if the person will survive or die...Let's go there...Let's go there today; Christmas is a beautiful day to make this visit. Showing love to other people, we pray for them in the ER, in the hospital chambers.

If you want you can go to the other countries. If you want go even further. You who are lonely now in your bed. Make a prayer for the countries where the smokes of war still are. There, where war was a recent event–Lebanon, Iraq, Iran, Serbia–only a few years ago. These wounds haven't closed yet. We say that these events happened: These events happened, but has the orphanhood ended? Even if five or ten months have passed, or five and ten years. Destructions do not fade this way. The news on TV mentions it two or three days. The event has passed, we forget about it. But the pain is still there, the wound haven't closed. The bodies of the children are even more tortured. There are still children who are crying there, the orphans.

Go there and make a visit. And if you feel tired, stop, if you feel stuffy...and I'm sorry, turn off... turn off the radio, I won't ...I won't insist, I don't want to upset you, but I want to tell you that you have a p o w e r today! An enormous power, there where you are sitting alone. See the matter in a different way. See it from another perspective. Don't feel melancholic, but learn to love. Make a step this year in the area of love. Enter inside the arena of love. You are not being loved? You be the one to love them. They don't speak to you? You be the one to speak. They are not praying for you? You be the one to pray for the others. Why do you seek to receive? Learn to give! And you will see how great you will feel. It's a different way this one, difficult. It shakes up our ego, but, if we do this it is...It will achieve very much, we will be very happy.

So, you can handle this. You say ok! Since you can still stand it, let's make one more visit; let's make a visit...Let's leave a few sweets in the houses of the divorced ones, today, if you want. Today, in the houses of those who are divorced, we will leave some candies there also. A prayer, a soft touch;

sometimes we have to pull someone's ear (to be upset with him), and say : "How did you manage to end up this way?" Make a visit. Think a little: some people are spending Christmas this year alone, for the first time, without their wife, or the woman without her husband, without the children...because the children are with the ex-husband, the ex-wife, their grandmother. The family is broken. You who are on your own, have you thought about that? Make your prayer for them also, for the others who are on their own. Last year this day the family was together. They had their fights, they had other things to argue about, they said we will take a divorce, will...will and will. But "will" unfortunately for some became a fact, a reality. How do these people feel, that for the first time this year they will experience Christmas alone, being divorced, being tired...Won't they feel sorrow? How did they manage to reach this point? And their children, how do they feel? That their father and their mother aren't together this year, and will bring their presents to them, each one separately on a different day. That they have to eat with their mom and their grandmother, because in the afternoon their dad will ring the bell, to go down to him, in order to go and see Santa Claus and the Christmas tree. And then at night they will return back home...while last year they were all together, making a visit, eating all together and the house smelled good. While now the house brings sadness. You, who are a lonely person today, you don't have to live this kind of loneliness, isn't that right?

So, make a prayer for these people, for these souls, who are your brothers. And go, if you want, and make a visit to the prisoners, in prisons. Where it's prohibited to enter...The visiting hours are specific, from this time until that time. The bars are in the way. It is prohibited to.... Nothing is prohibited. For the prayer nothing is prohibited! Let's go everywhere, no one will bother us. We can go and sit as long as we want inside his cell, of the prisoner, of those on trial, but especially of the prisoner, who was convicted fairly or unfairly. Let us not be so happy, when the people who were convicted fairly enter prison, the really guilty ones...Aren't we really guilty in so many other things? We are all guilty. We are all guilty and sinners, even if we are out of jail. Some people are glad: someone goes to jail and they say: "I enjoyed it, the law was imposed, I got my revenge." Yes ok, but forgive me to say that what you just said deserves prison. Your revenge deserves prison from God. When God says: "You should love your enemies," love your enemies. When Christ says: "If you think something bad about someone, you have already done something bad inside you." How many of us haven't committed murders, haven't hurt, haven't upset in our soul the other. Ok, you haven't done a crime. It's a lot worse if you really do it, but it is also bad for God, who sees our heart, our intellect, our soul. He sees how guilty we all are. We are all guilty. We all deserve to go to prison. And now there are people in prison. And they have been humiliated in prison. And in prison they have apologised to God. And God has already forgiven them, even if the courts of the state haven't. And let them be imprisoned for a life sentence and twice a life sentence and as long as they want. But for God they are forgiven and free "for this and the future age." If they regret, if they confess, if they are forgiven...So, come on, be the one to make a prayer for them. And those of you who are prisoners and listen right now–because I had a call from there– make a prayer for those who have not understood the things that you understand now. I'm a prisoner, but inside the prison, at least...This is Christmas day!...A prisoner on Christmas. "Christ was born" and I'm in prison!! It's Christmas alright, but I'm in prison on Christmas, I know this name, I say this name, I love this name, and I know Christ.

There are many other prisoners, who are prisoners in Hades even if they are alive: they have no hope, they have nowhere to turn. You are in an advantageous position. Soltzhenitsin said, "Inside the prison I met freedom. Inside the prison I met Christ. I am in prison, but I'm happy. I found the truth inside the prison!" So, don't cry and the rest of you don't take it wistfully. You can also make the attack of love. The counterattack of love. And pray for us, the ones outside of the prison's walls. I feel more imprisoned. I feel that I am the one in prison, inside my ego, behind the bars of my passions, my wickedness, my jealousy, my gluttony, my sensuality, all of my passions. All of my passions that torture me. Aren't these bars? Isn't this a prison? You can get out of these bars: maybe you are inside the prison, but outside of the one I'm talking about. Please, make this gift to us, to me. Pray for me, as I'm a prisoner, maybe more than you. And if you can't do anything of the above, and if you find it difficult, or if you tried them and got tired or if you stopped doing them at some point, make a call. Make a call to a lonely person today. He is right now saying with his life: "Lord, I have no one." I have no one. And you say, you have no one? I'll keep you company today. I will keep you company for a few minutes, I'll call you to tell you something, to chat, to say "Hello," to tell you: "Don't be upset...we are together, my friend, life goes by, we will get through this. We will make it, God will not abandon us." Even if you are lying down, even if you are confined, paralysed, and so on. For example, Father Porphyrios was lying in bed sick and had a speaker phone and he was talking to the phone consoling people, and his word was travelling and gave warmth to the souls who listen to him.

So, this is very good. And the ones who have a big heart today...the ones who have reached the parking lot by now. You will park the car and get out. I see. You are arriving home, you are almost there. You have a big heart and a big Christmas table, if you have the strength and the space in your soul, invite a lonely person today, to come to your house. Tell him or her to come and join you for dinner. And I have experience of this situation, I have...and you know where? In the houses of families, who have many children! Isn't it unbelievable, parents with many children, families with seven children, with twelve children, thirteen children, with five children, being happy to invite extra people on Christmas day! And they also invite strangers, who are not related to them, but this day they have no one. And once I was invited along with others, complete strangers. And I said: "Excuse me, why do you invite these people, don't you feel sorry for yourselves?" I say this between us "What were you thinking, Please explain to me. So much trouble. So many tables, so much food and you also invite others? Let's say, how can you stand them all together?" "But," he says, "Father, today is Christmas, it's Easter, we will celebrate Christ's resurrection, you know, we are happy to have them at our table, our Christ says that. When you are going to dine, don't invite the decent people of your time and those who are going to tell you "thank you" and will return you the favour. Because if they return you the favor, you got your reward from the people. You should invite those who have nothing to give you back, but only their 'thank you,' only their tears of gratitude, only their endless love." And this coming from their heart. Very difficult, right? To invite to your Christmas table today, to the one you and your family barely fit, and say, you can come and eat, come let's eat all together, and all these people will fit together. Surprisingly, everyone fits. They fit! If you can and have time, if the food isn't ready yet, make a call, find someone that you know, that you want. But don't be misunderstood: invite him with a courteous soul, with courage! Invite him, Christ says so:

"You are inviting Christ." What a great thing for someone to do!

So.... so today is Christmas! A very beautiful day. A very beautiful day, a festive day, a happy day! In the end, we did many things, we the lonely ones. We made many visits. And will make even more until tonight, make prayers, visits, phone calls, conversations. You are able to do that from your position. I wish the lonely people today to have strength, resistance and faith: faith in Christ's love. Be strong. Be strong you who are alone in your life. Don't cry. Don't feel melancholic. Because this feeling hides an ego in your heart. "Why do I not have something? Why has life treated me this way? Why? ..." These thoughts indicate ego. No...It's what God wanted! See it with humiliation and power. Take strength inside your soul. You should stand still! In this way, the rich will feel even richer in their heart and in their love. Let them be rich in there. And let us all feel together with this happiness of the celebration...to feel, my brothers, also a little regret. Ok, we will be happy, we will sing, but inside this endless happiness of Christmas, let's feel also a little regret, let's feel a little sad.

You know why? Because this holy day there are still teary eyes in this world. There are teary eyes even in our building where we live, in our neighborhood. There are teary eyes and you know it. You know it: across your street someone lives with a pain in his heart. You know that across your street someone lives who is married with a very difficult woman, a difficult child, who is looking for a job. Someone lives across your street who ... you know those things. There are still teary eyes. And in the entire world! And can I tell you something? Tonight, if we can, we will experience a lonely moment—we are all going today to experience at least one– when we go to our room to sleep, to rest after the impressions of the day are over, all the trouble of the day... (Ah! Now you can listen about these things, even at night! You know, the show is airing also at night. Usually on Monday night). Now you will listen to the show, and then it will be over. You are going to sleep at some point. This day will end. In the end, we are all going to be alone. We are all alone in this world. The married and the unmarried ones, the families who have many children. Because, in the end, everyone sleeps alone with himself. It's just himself alone and his God.

So, when we are left alone, this day, if a tear runs from our eyes, such a happy day, a tear of regret, I think Christ will take it. This tear will not be wasted. He will take it and do you know what he is going to do with it? This beautiful day and this beautiful night, he will make it a star! He will make it a star to warm that cold earth of ours, and this star will shine in the sky of the world. Because it will be a tear of love! Let's pray this night, with great joy because Christ was born, and with great sadness, because we still haven't put Christ's birth in our heart. And Christ will unite our tear with His own, His child tears, His infant tears. But even now, maybe tears are running from His eyes! Because, because it's not yet a reality what He said: "Glory to God in the highest, and on earth peace, good will towards men." Christ was born, the Angels praised God, but peace still hasn't come to earth. The Lord is giving us peace. Those of us who want Him, those of us who extend our hand and touch Him and accept Him inside us, those of us who commune with our Christ these days, we have the Lord and His peace inside us. But this peace hasn't been spread everywhere. There are still souls who haven't received Christ. There are still souls who feel sadness, loneliness, emptiness, sorrow. For t h o s e souls, then, let's allow to drip from our eyes–yes, this is how special this day is– it's ok–, when we are alone, a tear of love, of goodness, of warmth! A tear that will go and ease the pain of others.

Well, my brothers, my sister and my lonely brother, you who are alone, remember: **you are not alone**! Near your bed, in your room, in your cell there is Christ. You live for Him; He came to this world today for you! To console you! Merry Christmas! And if you haven't eaten yet, bon appetit! With the sweet joy of Christmas in your hearts, in your eyes, in your soul. So that your house will be filled with the happiness of Christmas, and the love of the great God, who became a small infant, so that we can get close to Him, to tell Him our pain, our sorrow, and to be consoled by His loving hands, that will bless us today, and throughout our lives!.

Merry Christmas, dear listeners of the church of Piraeus! We will meet again at the next show! May the God of love be with you. Goodbye!

BACK FROM MOUNT ATHOS

Translation by Ioanna Alexaki

---

*"...I also went to Mount Athos last year
and when I was kissing the icon of the Lord's Mother,
I don't know why, but I felt like crying..."
T.M. Lamia (e-mail)*

I went for a few days to Mount Athos again. I went away for four or five days to clear my mind, to calm down, to relax and rest. To find myself, to get in touch with my God a little again, and now I am back.

I thought to use this opportunity and instead of commenting on some familiar theme, to tell you some fresh news I have. Fresh memories and impressions from my short journey and pilgrimage to Mount Athos, would you like that?

I'll tell you about a few things that impressed me. These days that I spent without a phone, e-mail, television or radio, magazines or newspapers were very meaningful to me because basically it cleared my mind. My soul was truly quieted down. It was a very nice experience being away from all this barrage of modern media technology, a kind of detoxification. From what I am telling you, you realise that we no longer live a normal life in this world.

You should not feel jealous when you hear that and think that I have the opportunity to achieve that and you do not. It is not easy. Obviously we also must take our leave and we leave behind obligations, people who need us, but it cannot be done otherwise. You cannot let yourself be dissolved within this world. You need to rest and it is necessary for all of us to be able to find some personal time. Others may want to go to Mount Athos or to some other pilgrimage to find the tranquillity of their souls; others may find peace of mind in their country house or elsewhere. What is important is not where you go but finding and using time appropriately in order to restore the serenity of your soul.

The Lord Himself, when His disciples returned from a missionary tour that He had sent them, told them: 'Come ye, and rest a little', 'you can come and relax a bit now'. Man truly needs this rest, and only when he has experienced it, he understands how unnatural our life has become in the city. How sick the mind is from the constant barrage of news, facts, information... We go mad and we do not even realise it.

What is even worse is that we reach a point where we think we actually need this madness and we feel that we cannot do without it. And I ask you: Did anything bad happen to me during those days when I did not watch any TV? When I did not watch any news nor learn about any new events? What I did, without knowing what was going on in the outside world, was pray for the world, saying the following prayer: "Lord, Jesus Christ, have mercy upon Your world." I did not know about the current events and developments. But I think there was no reason to know the details, since they are already familiar to me: persistent problems, wars, economic crisis, worries, diseases, earthquakes, wrecks. Don't we know all this already? Are they not always the same, constantly recurring? We hear about them here, but we do nothing! We hear about them, but we do not pray. At least there on Mount Athos although I would not hear about the news, I would not know about it, God would speak to me in my soul and in my heart and I would pray for all these people and all these situations.

Here in the city we hear about everything, but this knowledge touches our hearts and minds only superficially, and then it is lost, and we literally become sick. This life we are living, is not normal, it is not natural. Nothing is clear, neither the air we breathe nor the water we drink.

There, everything is pure and virginal, original, authentic and beautiful. Your lungs are cleansed; both the lungs of your heart and your body. You drink water and you feel cool because it is clear water, from gurgling sources which descend from the mountains. And the air... you really feel you are breathing oxygen! You breathe the salty air from the sea. You look at the sea and your eyes stare at the horizon, you rejoice with all your heart! Wherever you look around you here, all you see is apartment buildings, columns, and gray asphalt. Here, you constantly hear noises that annoy you and do not allow your soul to calm down; while there, there is an infinite calmness. The birds sing their sweet chirp; the monks do their jobs quietly, their ministries without stress or pressure, in calm, human rhythms. What a nice thing that was! Honestly, I liked it so much and now that I have returned, I admit that this whole situation did me good. It was good for me to keep my cell phone switched off; the cessation of messages and phone calls was so beneficial, so liberating.

This liberation helps you to find your real self again. And it is very beautiful to become ourselves again, the way that God created us, and placed us within the calm rhythms of nature.

Do not think that I was able to enjoy all these things for a long time; it was only for four or five days. However, it was not the duration that made the difference, but simply, the fact that there you have the potential to realise your soul's serenity. The benefit you get from that experience is so strong that it leaves a mark in your heart, a mark of serenity and calmness.

One evening I decided to go to the Liturgy so I got up at three o'clock, before dawn – something which is unthinkable by the rhythms I live here. I looked at the sky and it was full of stars, beautiful stars that you cannot see here in the city because of the smog. And because, of course, you do not get up at this hour, since there is no motive for you to do so. But there these people are different, they are people who pray! And their motivation to get up in the middle of the night is a group of people which consists of 40, 50, or 60 Fathers, depending on the monastery that they choose to go to, and one influences the other, and one spreads his enthusiasm to the other, and they are all carried away into collective action! No, there no one can feel alone, or think individually. You see them in their cells bending their knees and praying for the whole world and you say, 'What, am I going to be lazy? It is not possible to do that!' and spontaneously, and most importantly voluntarily, of your own will, you move with their rhythms, because you see the flame of prayer alive in front of you. You are encouraged, and even if you are lazy and indifferent, you wake up a little and you say: 'I want to pray also, like everyone else.'

It was a very beautiful Liturgy! That night I saw great people, saints, and only thinking of them gives me strength. And I thank them from the bottom of my heart, and I feel so grateful for the fact that they exist and they pray. They may never build apartment buildings, or do any of the tasks that people see and appreciate today, but what they do is grand, and only by thinking about it, I feel resurrected, awakened and I want to become a better person, I want to do something also.

There I saw an old hermit. A monk, who had been on Mount Athos for 50 years without ever leaving, not even to go to another monastery. He does not go to celebrations, masses or vigil masses except in his own monastery. He has stayed for 50 years in the same unique place, in the place where he got to know God, and he keeps repeating the same prayer. He claims that this is the gift that God gave him, to commemorate constantly and continuously the name of Jesus Christ. And he says: 'Lord Jesus Christ, have mercy upon me' continuously, day and night. And in this place he has gotten to know everything, where God is, and within God he has found the whole world. He feels the whole world in his heart and he does not need to move. People come to see him, literally to see him, because he does not speak, he does not have any kind of conversation. He will rarely discuss anything with you and usually he avoids speaking about his experiences.

He told me, however, that he was taken once to Thessaloniki, because he had fainted while he was chanting, and he was taken to be examined by the doctors to make sure he was alright. So essentially he got out of the monastery without being aware of it, because otherwise he would never have wanted to leave. Then he asked me to say a prayer for him since I am a priest and he is "just" a monk. He asked me to pray, that the next time I visit that specific monastery for him not be there, for Christ to have taken him to be with Him. And he was saying that and he was happy, content, really desiring life at the side of Christ. 'Look,' he said to me, 'how many years are we supposed to live? What is the purpose of our life? Isn't it to come closer to Christ? I love Him and talk to Him all day. I want to meet Him and this is going to be my happiness! I wish He would take me to be at His side, now that I am going back to my cell. There is nothing more beautiful than leaving in order to be close to Christ whom you love.'

In that moment I realised that the rest of us do not want to leave because we do not love Christ and we think that life is beautiful. We like the TV channels, the series, the programs, the trips, and the food. This is the life that has captivated us, has stolen us. We have been seduced by this world and we have grown roots. However, that monk has not made that mistake; he has not been captivated by this material world. He lives here in his body but his soul is somewhere else. His heart is already in Heaven. What a human being!

He also told me that I should take part in communicating this message. That I ought to motivate people to pray and say this prayer: 'Lord Jesus Christ, have mercy upon me' to ask Christ, to say His name and to call upon His Grace. Then I expressed my disappointment for the fact that I was leaving Mount Athos, and he explained to me that wherever I go Christ is always going to be at my side, because He is everywhere. 'Listen,' he said, 'I will tell you what to do. You are going to go home, you are going to draw the curtains, and you are going to feel that you are here. And do what you would do if you were here. Would you pray here? Do the same there. You can. Would you fast? Do the same there. Would you stay up all night praying? Stay at home all night praying. If you were reading a spiritual book here, read it also at home. Draw the curtains and do not think that you are in your house, in Athens, because it does not matter where you live, but how you live.'

What a beautiful thing! 'Draw the curtains and do whatever you were going to do here.' It is not difficult! It is easy and it is real! And if I think in my mind that I am there, what would I be doing? There, I wouldn't have any anxiety, so I must try and do the same here. It is something that I can control. There, I wouldn't be anxious or in a hurry; I can be the same here also. There, I would not be on the phone all day, so I can be here also without the phone and decide that for a few hours or for a few days I will not speak and that I will live in peace and quiet. I can do that, as long as I try to detach myself from all these habits that cause me anxiety.

The things I am telling you may cause you to feel what I would call a well-intended envy of the place where these holy people live, like the monk I just mentioned. Generally it is not nice to feel envy. We certainly can feel well-intended envy of Christ and the Saints, but we must not envy locations, because it is as if we are saying to Christ that He is not with us in some specific places, while the Lord is present everywhere. It is as if we are saying to Him: 'Lord, in this place where I live, you are being unfair to me.' It is as if we are saying to Christ that His behaviour is unfair, that His providence and care of the world is not equal. No, this is a serious mistake, because Christ is everywhere. His love is everywhere and wherever we are. And we can do so many things for Him also.

There was another old Father with whom we started talking about my radio programme, which he listens to. This monk is not used to listening to music. 'I want to listen to preaching,' he said to me, 'and you have music. Say that to the person responsible for the music, please.' I replied that people in the cities nowadays are not used to the life of hermits like the monks on Mount Athos and they cannot endure speech alone. So we decorate speech with something that is more relaxing and easier to receive, like music, so that speech can enter our minds more softly and touch our souls. 'I do not know of such things,' he said, 'I want to listen only to speech.' But the truth is that music, for us tired city people of the 21st century, is something that we really need because it comforts us. Besides, there must be music also in Heaven. Music of the angels and we simply do not know what it is like.

At some point during our conversation, this Father asked me if I ever feel embarrassed during my radio programme, due to the fact that many people are listening to me as I speak. 'Do you not become confused, when people look at you and listen to you?' he asked me. I told him that he was right and that certainly I get confused sometimes, but when I see the people's love and response, I gain courage and strength because I do not feel like I am talking to strangers, but to people who love me. I do not go out to some square to address people who do not want to listen to me, who do not believe and who will laugh at what I am saying or mock me. I go out and I talk to people who are my brothers and sisters and my friends, who are Christians. People who struggle more than I do and who embrace me with their prayers and their love, and that makes my fear go away. He wondered and said that it would be very difficult for him to do that. Then I did not neglect to confess to him that his prayer had helped me a lot in what I do, and that that was my secret. Some time ago at Mount Athos, this same person had said to me: 'Speak Mr. Supervisor,' that is how he called me, 'Speak, because the Lord has made you a priest for a reason, to address the faithful and inform them of His will. So whenever you are invited to speak, do it, get involved and attend to that occasion.' And this is how things have turned out!

Another incident that happened during my stay at Mount Athos is the following: I went to another monastery where I met an 18-year-old student who had just finished high school and was there as a would-be novice monk, which means he was there to try and see whether he could stay on Mount Athos. 'What are you doing here?' I asked him. 'I am a novice monk,' he replied. 'I came here to test myself, to see if I can endure, to try and be tried,' because this is what being a novice monk means. He who tries in order to find out whether he likes that particular way of life, but who at the same time is also tried in front of others if he can become accepted by them and coexist with them. Which means that through this procedure you see whether you can stay, but also whether the others can keep you, so nothing is certain or taken for granted. You go, you try, you see, you do not commit, and you are not obligated. You can choose to leave, you can choose to stay. This is a preparatory stage and a trial period to find out whether he who goes to Mount Athos can stay.

Someone told me that he considered this young man's action as totally immature and superficial, due to the fact that he was only eighteen years old and could not make appropriate decisions. I considered this belief totally wrong and I gave him an example: When my mother got married she was only 19 years old and the fruit of that marriage was me, who later in life became a priest. So according to my interlocutor's point of view, my mother's action which resulted in my being born, was immature! When I gave him that example he reconsidered his point of view regarding immaturity and gave me the impression that he had understood.

Of course, I know many people who got married at a very early age and have regretted it. There are moments in our lives when we make decisions based on enthusiasm that we may later regret. But there are also cases where the opposite is true. No one knows what will happen in the future. So the best thing we can do – as far as marrying at a young age is concerned – is not to say anything and not to criticise or judge, which is what a lot of people do. However, when we see someone who wants to dedicate themselves to God at a young age, our opposition is so much more intense!

To tell you the truth, in all those years that I have known students, children who have finished high school, it was the first time that I met a young person who chose to go to Mount Athos at such an early age. For me this is an exception, a very beautiful and blessed one indeed, which shows that even to this day God inspires souls and places within the hearts of young children the desire to love Christ so much. So I cannot understand why this is considered to be so bad and why my interlocutor reacted so negatively to this young person's decision. In the end, no one can know what is hidden in each person's heart.

This discussion brought to my mind Father Porphyrios who was only 12 years old when he went to Mount Athos. Today, everybody reads his books and learns about his life. People are touched and moved to repentance by the miracles he performs! This may be the exception to the rule, but no one knows if, for example, the 18 – year – old student I mentioned before will be another exception!

I am totally convinced that these things belong to God. If it is God's will for something to happen, it will happen. And again, if something is not God's will, it will not happen even if the world turns upside down. This means that, even if someone wants to become a priest and it is not God's will, it will not happen. He will have, for example, obstacles in his path, and if he is well-intended he will realise that and will stop. I refer to good intentions, because many times people do things only because of stubbornness and then, most of the time, the results are negative. You may, for example, become a monk only because of stubbornness, and to oppose the will of someone else. You may do the same thing also in the matter of marriage. That is why we see so many unhappy marriages, because many people get married without really knowing why. Maybe this decision was not God's will, maybe in their heart they felt that they wanted to devote themselves to God, but they did not know the way because no one ever talked to them about this perspective. It was considered impossible, maybe even unnatural or unusual!

And yet, God has given to many people the inclination to devote themselves to Him. But this is something which is not cultivated in our times. No one comes today to inspire young people to give themselves to God. What a beautiful thing and how easily and arbitrarily we criticise and judge it! The best thing that could happen is that there are people who are praying for the whole world! People who would be experiencing what Starets Panthenios experienced in Russia, a holy hermit who said one day to the Virgin Mary: 'Holy Mother, what is the meaning of my becoming a monk? What is the meaning of what I did? Tell me the secret.' And the Virgin Mary answered: 'Do you want to know what the meaning is? It means that you must sanctify yourself for the sake of all humanity! You must become an offering for all humanity.'

I think of these things sometimes... when I cannot sleep, and at the same time there are Fathers at Mount Athos who stay up praying so that I can go to sleep! When I am sick in a hospital, or drowning in my sins, in my poverty, in my problems, they are praying for me. So why is it so bad for people to devote themselves to God? I will admit that I was so touched when I saw a young boy trying to put himself through trials in order to devote himself to God, and I am certain that there are more like him. I do not know what he will do eventually, but this is not the point.

Many people believe that if a person goes through the trial period to become a monk and after a while has second thoughts about it and leaves, that he is a loser. Personally, I do not consider that as failure but as a blessing from God in this person's life. It means that for a specific period of time, no matter how long it was, he had this sacred desire in his heart, and that is a blessing regardless of the fact that in the end he did not manage to achieve it. I will always remember that this person desired to rise higher, to touch the top. He set a sacred, blessed and divine goal. Is that bad? At least he tried, he realised how much he could endure and he realised that he could not reach that level, and he said humbly 'I cannot do this' and he left. It is not to be scorned; on the contrary it is commendable, even if was only for a short while.

Most people want futile things. Someone sets as his life's purpose to buy a specific type of car and so he saves money for that. Is that a purpose that will give meaning to his life? And yet he does that and no one scorns him. Someone else sets a goal to go and watch the Olympic Games. Is that a life's goal? I do not blame him, but surely I cannot place him on the same scale as the one who has as his life's purpose to love Christ and devote himself wholeheartedly to Him.

I learned from this young man. Every day, or I would rather say every night, he would get up at dawn to attend midnight Mass to pray. I watched him obey, offer, work, help, serve the visitors. This voluntary work is so beautiful. Generally, within the church, beautiful things happen which remain unknown to many. Unknown, because television never shows them since something like that does not result in high ratings.

There in the monastery I met another person who touched me with what he told me about his life. He recounted that he had been on a missionary trip to Africa – I do not remember where exactly, maybe in Zaire – and while he was there he was notified from the monastery that he had to go back, because there were certain needs that required his help. Despite the fact that he loved being a missionary very much and he loved what he was doing, he returned without any delay. The reason he did that was that, as far as monks are concerned, obedience comes above all else. 'We obey our Spiritual father,' he said to me, 'we do not have the right to say 'I want this' or 'I demand,' and we do not have any kind of attachment, to want something so intensely that we cannot let go of it. We are not like that. We can endure anything and everything. We can also let go of anything and everything if we are asked to. I will admit father, that I liked the mission very much. You see people listening to you with their eyes and ears wide open, absorbing the words of Christ in amazement. You see people of all ages being baptised. You see them burn the books about magic. There I really saw the thirst of people and the effectiveness of the Evangelical word upon these souls. Your heart rejoices. You rejoice in offering for the glory of Christ. You love people and people love you. You bond with them and suddenly you are called back to your monastery in Greece, and you must go back... So, I left everything and I returned.' Obviously, I asked him when he was going to return to the mission and he replied that he was not going to return because he was needed at the monastery. I thought I detected some sadness on his face so I tried to comfort him by telling him not to be sad. But he said: 'I am not sad, I am simply talking about it,' and he was calm and serene.

Then I tried to put myself in his position and I thought that if they had done something like this to me I would be sad. What thing? To cancel a wish of mine, to destroy a plan and instead of doing what I wanted to do something that someone else wanted. And yet this monk said to me: 'It does not matter; I do not have any plans.' 'But didn't you like it there!' 'I did like it, but now I am going to like whatever new you are going to tell me.' And he was indeed very calm and serene, accepting without any objection or sadness what he had to do.

He was the first person who came to my mind when, returning from Mount Athos, I received a call from a woman who said that she kept fighting with her husband because neither of them could do something for the sake of the other and neither of them was willing to cancel their plans. It is terrible, isn't it? What the monks experience daily as struggle and spiritual exercise, as a reality in their life, most of us cannot even imagine, let alone do. The monks do not have any demands. This humility, this readiness to change, to soften their soul, to be flexible, not to be rigid and demanding, is great. If we could do that in the city, the couples would be very happy. The families would be joyful. One would compromise for the sake of the other.

I was taught a great deal from this monk's experience. I think that what he did was to continue his mission on a different level now. The message that comes out to the Fathers of Mount Athos and the world is that this monk returned not because he disliked some people, or because he fought with someone, or did not endure, but because above all he wanted to satisfy God's will expressed through his spiritual father. This is a great offering, a great mission. And that teaches me now: essentially he extends his mission to me. And although he is not on a mission in Africa, he is still a missionary, because he teaches humility, obedience, the love of God, and sacrifice.

Leaving myself in the hands of God means I trust, I am calm. The saints advise us to be like a sphere which rolls on the ground and goes everywhere because it has no edges and cannot get stuck anywhere. It rolls and it goes. This is what this person has achieved. He is like a sphere in the hands of God and he goes to where he is directed by Him without any reaction. He is like a leaf in the autumn driven by the wind and taken to wherever the wind blows. It stops in a certain place and when the wind blows again it moves along without any objections, without any demands, it does not go contrary to the breath of God, contrary to the breath of the wind. The monks live exactly like that.

We are talking about the good monks, though, because if someone does not want to struggle, even if he is in a monastery, he may have objections and may try to implement his own will one way or another.

But now we are referring to someone who really wants to struggle. And I am not lying to you, there was calmness on this person's face all the while he was recounting his story, a calmness that I did not have. I envy that; I would like to be like that if and when something is cancelled in my life. Because when you do something for God, you must not get attached to what you are doing but to the essence of it, that you are doing it for God. In simple terms, I could put it like that: I want to do something for You. If You want me to go on a mission, I will do it, not because it is a mission but because I will be doing this for You and I will get joy out of the fact that it will satisfy You, because through this I will show my love to You. If I know that You want me to get on a plane and fly back (the monk told me that he took all his belongings and went back), I will love You. For me the question is to love You, it does not matter how.

I remember once I was on my way to give a speech but the organisers had made a mistake and had not informed the people about the specific date. While I was walking down the road I was feeling happy since I did not know what had taken place. However, I cannot tell whether I was happy because I was going to talk about Christ or because I was going to make a speech. These are two completely different things. It is one thing to be going only for the glory of God and it is another thing to be going because you are satisfied with what you doing. So I arrived at the specific location and there was no one there. They will come, I said to myself, it cannot be otherwise. After a while a priest showed up and explained to me what had happened and that no one was coming. In that moment I felt as if I had fallen from the clouds, I was annoyed and disappointed. Of course I did not show how I felt. I simply said that it was fine and that mistakes happen. But within me I knew it had annoyed me. If I really loved God and only Him, I should have said: 'Lord, this is the way You wanted it and this is the way it happened.' And maybe I should have thought about something even more real, that God wanted to protect the people from my words which would have been full of selfishness, self-centeredness and self-projection. He did not want them to hear a polluted speech from a speaker who was not humble, because at that time I would have spoken for me and not for Him. This is the real truth but I did not think of it like that then.

So this monk taught me when he cancelled his desires. And other monks taught me by their humility, because there is a lot of humility on Mount Athos. At times I think of the Fathers who are there and I am so moved. You see figures wrapped in black and you do not know who the person who passes you by is, and you do not recognise him. What is amazing about this is that he does not care if you recognise him or not. He is someone who loves Christ and nothing else, someone who is sent to you to show you Christ and nothing else. They seem as if they are saying to you: 'Does it matter who I am, what my name is, how old I am, what I have studied? Do not care about any of this. I live for Christ. If you want to know something about me, you should know only that I pray.'

A monk told me once: 'If you want to know something about me, it is only this. If you open my heart right now, you will find the name of the Lord Jesus Christ carved in golden letters. Know this; I do not want you to know anything else about me.' That teaches me, it moves me. They are humble figures, they have blessed faces, holy, beautiful, just like God wants them.

One day as we were all together around a dinner table at Mount Athos, I was looking across from where I was sitting at some workers who were eating. They were there helping with some construction work in the monastery. I saw someone who was wearing a hood like the ones young children wear when they go skiing in the mountains. He was looking at me. Because he was wearing the hood I could not see his face clearly so I could not tell who he was. But I was certain that he was looking at me and that I knew him from somewhere.

Many months before, here in Athens, I had seen a mother I knew here in church. I asked her how her son was, since I had not seen him for years. She burst into tears! She said: 'Haven't you heard?' I said: 'Heard what?' 'My son has become involved in drugs.' I felt as if I was hit by lightning! I knew this young man. He was a happy creature, a blessed child, with a pure, angelic face. After the Liturgy ended I waited to greet this woman before I left and one thought was tormenting me. So while I was talking to her I asked her to give me her son's phone number so I could talk to him. She answered that it was impossible to find him because the only possible place he could be, would be Omonoia square. 'Will he talk to me?' I asked her. 'I do not know if he will recognise you. If his mind is clear enough to be able to communicate...'

So I went to Omonoia square and I looked for quite a while among many drug addicts. Some were taking drugs, others were falling on the pavement, and others were sitting there immobile under the influence of the substance they had used. I looked here, I looked there, I passed discretely from one alley to the other, but I did not find the person I was looking for. So I started to worry and I was praying to God to bless this child, I was praying for him to be safe.

So here I am now on Mount Athos, sitting at the dinner table in the monastery looking at the workers across the table from me as I mentioned earlier, and I recognised the stranger who was looking at me, it was that boy! In the beginning he did not recognise me either. On his way out of the dining room he passed in front of me. I had not seen him in six or seven years and in the meantime he had gotten mixed up with drugs. As soon as I realised who he was, I stopped him at once! I said to him: 'Is that you?' He said: 'Father?' And he kissed me. He kissed me as he would kiss his father, on the cheeks, not like you would kiss the hand of a priest in respect, because these kids need care and love and warmth, they miss these things. Although he had the love of his family, generally for people like him who are in pain, such feelings are always more than necessary. He held my hand and would not let go! And his hand was shaking, shaking... I do not know from what... I do not know why... These people may have damaged their nervous system by all this abuse... Anyway, he was sensitive and his hand was shaking as if he was an old man. I could feel it in my palm and he would not let me go. I asked how he was and he replied: 'Haven't you heard...?' 'I have,' I said, 'and I am very glad to see you here. Why are you here?" 'I came here and I am trying to get help from the Virgin Mary. I pray, I go to Masses, I help with the work and I am trying to detoxify myself, to calm down, to overcome it. Sometimes I go back to Athens, I get involved again and I come back here... I fall, I get up...' I was moved and I said to him: 'Know that God and the Virgin Mary will not leave you. You have got a path in your life. No one knows the end of your path. Do not be disappointed. Do not despair! Do what you can and I am so glad that I saw you here. A few months back I was looking for you in Omonoia square and today I see you here in the arms of the Virgin Mary, in Her Garden...! The young man was moved by my words and asked me what time my boat was leaving, because he wanted to spend some time with me to tell me what he had not been able to all these years!

Indeed he came to see me before I left – because I was leaving in a few hours – and he brought me pictures of his family, of his loved ones. We talked and he seemed moved! He was looking at me all the time and he asked me to pray for him. He kissed my hand again. He had this strong desire to feel warmth, love and caring, fatherly and motherly caring at the same time.

In that moment a thought crossed my mind, that as I soon as I arrived in Athens I would go to the reporters of the TV channels who criticise and comment negatively about the monasteries of Mount Athos, and tell them to go and interview this young man! So that he can talk to them about the church and the monks, about how he felt near those people and that he could take his life back into his own hands and seek the serenity of his soul! To make them understand how he found meaning and purpose on Mount Athos and how if he had not gone there he might have committed suicide, or gone crazy! This is Mount Athos; these are the things that are not known. This is what it offers, what will not be heard on TV, on the channels simply because these things do not sell!

Due to the need for constant viewing and high ratings, scandals, improper actions, and sinful things need to keep coming to the surface. Certainly someone might say: 'Why? Don't these things happen?' Yes they do, but there is also the other side, the beautiful elements, sainthood, health within illness, offering within weakness, love, a warm embrace, caring towards those who suffer and seek to find their path, the path of God. These things are not mentioned and for that I blame the journalists. This is Mount Athos, the place I loved, the place that touched me and the place from which I left full of happiness, strength, comfort, emotion and devoutness. Someone had told me once: 'Every time I go to Mount Athos I bring back with me something special.' Indeed he is right. Every time I go to Mount Athos I also bring back with me different experiences, which make me think about things, and make me become a better person.

Another incident which remains carved in my memory from this short trip took place at the airport. I was flying from Thessaloniki to Athens because I had booked this trip several months earlier and the ticket was cheap. I mention this because some people are tempted when they hear that a priest is travelling by plane, they think that he paid hundreds of Euros and they criticise him. No, it was a cheap ticket which cost only 35 Euros! Anyway, at the airport I was approached by a German couple, they were strangers to me, and they showed me a small box which contained two wedding rings. They were talking to me in German and I barely understood what they were telling me. The point was that they wanted me to bless their wedding rings! I was astonished by their request and I asked them if they were of the Orthodox faith. They replied that they were not and that they could not understand why they had to be in order for a priest to bless them and they were right! I accepted with great pleasure and the couple was very thankful and they left extremely touched!

After that incident I sat and thought a lot! I had just left Mount Athos so touched by all that I had experienced. And there I was at the airport and the only thing I wanted to do was withdraw within myself and think of all the beautiful things I had experienced. Then suddenly as if he was drawn to something, someone came to me and asked me to bless him for the 50th anniversary of his wedding. And this happened after I had left Mount Athos! In that moment I felt in my soul as if I had come somewhat closer to God, that when you truly go towards God, even for a little while, other people feel it deep in their souls and they want to come near you without you seeking it, without it being your intention! Only because you have been a person of God, even for a little while!

Then, after I had arrived in Athens, I took the subway to go home. A drug addict came in and he took out some papers and started saying what they usually say in similar situations, that he had been in rehabilitation, that he appeared on TV and that he needed help. In that moment I thought that it was impossible for me not to give him any money, so I gave him a few coins. A gentleman who was standing next to me asked why I did that, since it was certain that the young man would definitely spend that money to buy drugs. I really wondered! It is God who gives us life! Aren't we all addicted to one thing or another? When we spend so much time daily watching television, are we not addicted? When we spend so many hours talking on the phone, is that not a dependency? And what do we do about it? Does God punish us? Certainly not! Then why would I punish this young man? Besides, by giving half a euro I did not show him the way to drugs! I gave him love! Because a priest is love, he is caring and giving. And, instead of leaving, there in front of all the people in the compartment, he kissed my hand. He kissed the hand of a priest who had returned from Mount Athos, a fact that no one knew. But God knew and He talked to the soul of this young man telling him that in front of him was a priest, and that beneath his sins he could find the grace of Christ. Christ, who is love and who is the only one the world needs.

This is what Mount Athos showed me, that if you are a person of God, you have a lot to give. Even if you are sitting in the subway, or going to work, even if you are not doing anything, simply the fact that you exist, that you are breathing, you scent the name of Jesus Christ. The only thing you have to do is say the prayer: 'Lord, Jesus Christ, have mercy upon me' It is a big help, it is a big offering, to do that and then just let people act as they like. One will come to approach you, another will come to talk to you, and someone may react in order to see your reaction, to see if you are real. What they are all looking for is Christ. It is a beautiful thing to be Christians, Christ is a great honour.

I hope I haven't tired you with my stories. Deep down they are not only mine, they are yours as well, they are ours, they are of our church, and they are the wonders and magnificence of our Christ. And this is what we priests should do, remind you of the magnificence of God so that our hearts are comforted and we gain strength. May you all be blessed and may the grace of our Virgin Mary, the grace of all the Fathers of Mount Athos, of all the Saints of the churches of Mount Athos be with you, blessing and protecting your lives. May the Virgin Mary help us all understand that every place is Mount Athos, every place is a holy place, that every house, every room can be our personal Holy Mountain and that in the end what we are looking for is Christ, the Virgin Mary and the Saints, the comfort that the church provides, which is so warm and so real.

EASTER

Translation: Eleni Poulakou

"We have been at this hospital before when my brother was doing therapy, as he had been diagnosed with brain cancer. After several months filled with insufferable pain, our brother left this world. One night the doctors had told him he had another two days to live. Then, in one of the rare occasions that he burst into tears thinking of the baby he was leaving behind, he started chanting: 'Christ is risen from the dead, by death He conquered death, and to those in the graves He granted life!'. We came home on Saturday, on Sunday he received Holy Communion and he had already begun travelling until Monday, when he reposed. During his last days he cried ceaselessly and he was saying only one word: 'I love you'..."
K. & L.E. Crete (e-mail)

"Chist is risen from the dead, by death He conquered death, and to those in the graves He granted life!"

Why shouldn't I chant along too? I'll sing it, even though I don't have a good ear, even though I'm no music master, even though my voice is not so beautiful... We all, brethren, can chant during these days, even though we're off-key; we can strain our voices and hoarsen through chanting, declaring that Christ Is Risen.

Christ is risen. This is the great miracle we're experiencing these days, the great joy of our souls. The Lord is risen. No more lies, no more pain; everything's past. The Holy Week went by, the Lord's Crucifixion is over, and now our Christ is at last glorious, resurrected, aglow and replete with light. A new sun emerged from this empty monument, from our

Lord's tomb. The Lord Is Risen. Christ is risen and this is the grand proof, the grand foothold of our faith. Christ is risen and He is living. There is no other way to account for the church's actuality, for the fact that church exists.

Why does the Church of Piraeus exist? Why do we exist? Why are you called as you're called? Why do you bear this name, Kostas, Vassilis, Georgia, Anastasia, Photis, Panagiota? Why are you called this way? In whose name were you baptized? In the name of a dead man? In the name of someone who does not exist? No, brethren. This is no lie. Our Lord is risen. Christ exists and He is alive. He conquered death, He conquered decay and He lives among us. This is our faith's grandeur. This is what all of us, together, experience during this period and that's why, from the Lord's Resurrection onwards and for the next fifty days, we sing it ceaselessly to Him. Even though we cannot fully believe it, since we still feel finite, since we are subject to decay and death, to this life's futility – and our minds cannot contain, unfortunately, the uncontainable, grand, unuttered mystery of the Lord's Resurrection.

Leave aside, these days, for a little while all Christianity's social elements of justice, equality, joint ownership, etc, and try answering this question: Do you believe in the Lord's Resurrection? Stop listening for a while to all those things the Lord is said to have taught about love. Stop paying attention to the countless books and magazines issued, containing sayings of wise men and women, including all the Lord's beautiful words about love, humility and prayer. All these are wonderful and I won't disagree with that, but you must bear in mind that all these are based on the magnificent event of the Lord's Resurrection, that this is their foundation. Because the Lord is alive, exists, and He has now conquered death and decay. He is not just someone who came towards us, who lived and died, just like every human being. The Lord is wholly alive and He will live for ever and ever. He came into this world at a certain moment and from then on He exists as God-Man in eternity. The Lord of the universe, my Lord, my God. Do you believe in this Christ?

What we're saying is not logical. It can not be explained in a logical manner. It is a supernatural miracle, one you can live with your heart, one you can touch at with your faith. It is a miracle that you can only approach with your heart and soul, with the entirety of your being, without being able to explain it away with logic. But, consider this. You cannot define everything in life based on logic. The "supra-natural" exist; it's another class of experiences, belonging to another world.

This experience, this miracle, this reality, is what our Holy Church brings out to us these days. We believe in the Lord's Resurrection, we live it, we feel it in our hearts; it makes our faces glow and we see it glowing on the faces and the souls of our brethren. Christ Is Risen. The Lord exists and He lives among us. If it was otherwise, if we didn't believe this, according to the Holy Apostles, we would be the most miserable creatures in this world, supporting something that is not valid and giving our lives for a lie.

It is no lie, it's a Truth, yet one that needs befitting recipients to be accepted. It needs befitting hearts, humble souls, reborn beings, honest people seeking truth with good intentions, people with a keen sense of honour, a generous soul and a noble heart, or else the meaning of the Lord's Resurrection cannot be conceived. The only thing being accomplished - if you don't have all the above - is that you eat, drink, and have a good time, because the Lord is risen and you are told to do so, though without feeling within your soul the gifts bestowed upon you thanks to His Resurrection.

Brethren, although we're living in an era of rationalism, of the reign of logic, of advancements in technology and in positive sciences, our Church still touches our hearts - but we must be careful. The modern rationalistic world has brought along a huge burst of occultism and of marked para-religion, but not of true theology. This happens because, when true religion (the use of the term 'religion' for our faith is rather permissive, because it is not essentially a religion, but a divine revelation) is not functioning properly, para-religion flourishes in its place. Today, people believe in supernatural stuff, having no logical explanation, such as magical supernatural phenomena, superstitions, signs of the zodiac, reading the cards or the coffee signs; nevertheless, they are not able to believe in Christ's Resurrection.

Close to half of you follow the daily astrological predictions and advice for the day, as shown on TV, radio or the magazines. Many of you stick with what the cards or the coffee signs tell you; you try to interpret your lives on the basis of pagan beliefs and you brush aside all logic, holding onto superstitions. Yet, despite this behavior, which is devoid of reason, you find it hard to believe in the Lord's Resurrection. Why? Because Resurrection will have us judged as persons. Resurrection brings us face to face with Truth and calls upon us to take a stand face to face with its reality; though such an attitude is poignant, serious and responsible, man is reluctant to adopt it. There are many who claim that it is very hard to deal with this truth, which reaches to touch our hearts, and attempts to change them - as opposed to all the rest, that do not affect our personal lives. Modern pagan beliefs do not compel us to conquer our egos and our passions; they do not teach us to humble ourselves, to love and to transform our souls, in order to be reborn as proper beings. Resurrection, on the other hand, if one believes in it, asks of us to change, to become better human beings - and this requires a personal struggle and will.

I reckon anarchists write certain very accurate stuff on walls. I once read a graffiti saying: If God exists, then we're all in trouble. I think this phrase perfectly accounts for why people today refuse to believe. God's existence does not make them comfortable, God's existence is not to their interest, because, if God exists, then we are doomed! If Christ risen exists, it means that He, Who lives, has a personal relationship to us. It means that He, Who lives, will come at a certain moment and He will judge us, you and me. He will come to verify our lives, to see how we've lived, how we think, how we move, and this is something we cannot stomach. That's why, if we believe in Christ risen, we shall have to prove it by changing our way of life.

Christ is risen, brethren. This is a fact that you experience, you believe, you feel at church, while receiving the Holy Light. "...Come receive light from the unwaning light and glorify Christ who has risen from the dead..." Right at that moment, your faces were glowing; your hearts were filled with relief, soothing hope and comfort stemming from the Lord's Resurrection, from belief in this Resurrection. For, how else could this faith have been propagated? How else could we speak of Him? Can it be that we speak, celebrate, sing and rejoice at a dead man, two thousand years after His death? Why should we do such a thing? For a lie? No. The Lord is alive, risen and existing.

How come the whole world is changed? How come twelve people changed our planet? How come so many millions are Christians? In who's name? In a dead man's name? The Holy Apostles did, indeed, change the world. But, how come those twelve simple men, these illiterate, insignificant men, were able to steel their souls with such strength? Whilst, when seeing the Lord being arrested on the Mount of Olives, they fled, frightened, abandoning Him – how come they were able to get rid of their fear and to transform their souls? What made Apostle Peter, who denied the Lord in front of a little girl, saying he didn't know Him, afraid to confess his faith, what made him finally speak of Him with unparalleled zeal and with burning ardour in his soul? If the Lord was a dead man, who would have been able to be transformed in such a way, in the name of a dead man? Who is He, Who gave them the power? Who is He, Who assisted them?

Blabbing fairy tales is way too easy. It is nice and amusing, especially if you have companions that get fascinated by your words. But, who were the Holy Apostles' adherents? Who followed them? They did not invite people to attach to an easy and fabulous life, full of leisure and prosperity. On the contrary, they spoke of a harsh life, they touched at the most sensitive parts of people's souls and oftentimes they told them truths that hurt and were not were not well-received. They did this, all the same. They exposed themselves to terrible hardships and dangers, because they felt that the Lord's Resurrection was a matter of life and death. If you don't believe this, you don't believe anything. If you just believe that the Lord was a good teacher, a good man Who said nice things, yet you don't believe in His Resurrection, then you're not a Christian.

A Christian is he who believes in the living Christ - Who came into our world, lived, preached, taught, worked miracles, helped people and martyred for His faith by dying on the Cross, was buried and rose from the dead, sending the All-Holy Spirit to the world, to enlighten us forever and ever. This is the Christ we believe in, and it may look like a fairy tale, but it's not. We have living proof for all this, in the Holy Apostles and in all the saints and martyrs through the ages, who, when they saw the sword hanging above their heads, were not afraid, but stood firm by their faith in the Resurrection and kept invoking His name. For we all understand that, at that very moment, when you see the sword hanging above your neck, at that ultimate moment, when your whole life passes in front of your eyes and you feel you're going to hit the ground, you cannot keep on telling fairy tales. If what you believed was but a fairy tale, you become unmasked and you admit it, like many people do, people who believe in a multitude of things, but deny everything before death, before pain, before danger and threat on their lives. But the Holy Apostles, on that ultimate moment of danger, felt that what they believed was so true, that they had to defend it, even if it cost them their lives.

It is easy speaking words, theories. But there may be a time when we are called upon to give our lives for the theories we profess – and if we exhibit endurance and strength; if we feel our souls filled with ineffable happiness; if we experience the truth of what we believe in (not due to fanaticism or to a morbid spiritual condition), then we are transformed and the whole world is transformed with us, because our lives acquire meaning and substance. It's the only thing that withstands time. This is what conquers death. This is what conquers the decay and futility of this world, the logic of modern era people.

Christianity was propagated through oceans of blood, the blood of those who believed in Christ's Resurrection. Other religions, such as Islam, are propagated through bloodshed too. But our Orthodox faith, the unequivocal faith in the True Christ, in the Lord Resurrected, was not propagated through other people's blood, but through the blood of the Christians themselves. We Christians shed our blood for what we believed in. For Christ Risen. We did not shed other people's blood to have our faith propagated. We did not kill other men, we did not sacrifice other humans; we sacrificed ourselves. Christians died for what they believed in, for Christ risen, because they felt that it was worth sacrificing themselves for Him.

The Lord is risen, He is living and existing. Consider all those movements that faded away with time. The number of men who came, spoke, preached beautiful things and found people who would follow them, people whose lives were affected. Still, nothing of all these lasted in time; after a short while, they died down, they perished like they never existed. Now, see how different things are when it comes to our Lord! When we thought everything was lost, everything was in fact beginning! When the Lord was crucified, Scribes and Pharisees and all those who decreed His death went crazy with joy, thinking that this troublesome affair was over, that things were settled. But this wasn't the case, for that's when this burst of love, the real spread of Christianity, began. Like a wide, impetuous river that came over and gave new birth to humanity, irrigating the world with Heaven's fresh waters. Humanity was transformed. By the Lord's martyrdom, a new world, a new reality is launched and risen. After the Lord's death and Resurrection, his followers, those who loved Him, became more numerous. The Holy Apostles, their wider circle, His disciples, those living in Jerusalem – and how many more? In the beginning, they were but a handful of people. After the Resurrection, Apostle Peter preached and five thousand people turned into believers all at once. They repented, and this current of love started spreading like a relay race of light and true faith to the edge of the world. How did this come about? How did this happen, if our Christ is not alive, if He is not risen, if He is not moving among us?

Some wonder about where the Lord's body may be. They say He is not risen and that all this stuff is nothing but a bunch of fairy tales. That His body was not found in the All-Holy Tomb, because it was simply stolen; therefore His Resurrection is automatically refuted. No, these are lies and propaganda of persons that have a vested interest in having people believe Christ's Resurrection is a lie and a fairy tale. Because fairy tales do not grant people the strength to resist against something, to believe in something and to tap into their inner power, in order to improve themselves as human beings and to fight against injustice in the world! Think of it as follows: even the most insignificant person, the most common person in the remotest village of our homeland and of the whole world, is placed in a grave, and his relatives know where his relics are being kept, because they care for him. So, as regards to our Lord, if the Apostles hadn't seen Him risen, wouldn't they preserve His body? Wouldn't we have a piece of His relics, some kind of physical remains of Him? Why would they hide His body – to pretend what? That His Resurrection was a lie? But we can carry this a little bit further. Why would they die in martyrdom, if there had been no Resurrection? Why would this Truth of Christ's Resurrection lead Saint Andrew to be crucified on an X-shaped cross at Patra? Why would he do that? Why would he waive his life, his convenience for a lie? Christ Is Risen. The Lord is risen and that's why the Holy Apostles did what they did. That's why they weren't afraid of anything, because they comprehended that this was His greatest Truth.

Our Lord's tomb in Jerusalem, the All-Holy Tomb, is the living proof of this Resurrection. The place from which the All-Holy Light emanates during the last twenty centuries, not only every Easter, but continuously – only we see it on Holy Saturday at noon, when it comes out in a manifest and panegyric manner. This particular monument is empty - and there never has been an empty monument of such value, as is the Lord's tomb. Never has there been a treasury so valuable, while void of its treasure, as is the Lord's tomb. A tomb's value lies in containing the dead man's body. We go, for instance, to the tomb of a relative - our father, our mother, our brother - and we sit there, because we feel this person's presence, we weep and we think about him or her. But when the dead gets evicted from the monument, when the removal of relics takes place, we no longer go to the tomb, because it is empty.

And yet, our Lord's tomb sees thousands of pilgrims everyday, people that go there and weep out of joy and gratitude. Are all those who kneel before the All-Holy Tomb foolish, because the tomb is empty? Of course not! That's the reason they worship - because it is empty! For, if it contained the Lord's relics, then it would have let us down, Christ would not have conquered death! He would have been subjected to death like the rest of us. But Life, and Light, consolation and Hope gushes from His All-Holy Tomb. Resurrection gushes from His All-Holy Tomb.

I have been at the All-Holy Tomb, as many of you must have too. The number of times one has visited the monument is not important. A single time suffices to stamp one's heart, to make his inner world melt, to generate a strange tingling in his heart. A little while ago I had a formidable experience, while visiting Jerusalem with a group of students, forty youths nineteen to twenty-seven years old approximately.

The All-Holy Tomb, or the Resurrection Temple, closes each day from seven-thirty in the evening till eleven at night, and no one is allowed to remain inside. The temple reopens at eleven o'clock for pilgrims to enter and attend the Matins and the nightly Holy Service. For you must know that the first daily Holy Service is performed every night, throughout the year, at the All-Holy Tomb. It begins at eleven o'clock in the night and it ends at about two o'clock before daybreak. If you wish to worship, you may have to queue up for one, two, or three hours, just to enter for a short minute, kiss the Tomb, express your gratitude and your pain, and then exit again. Believers enter in batches of three, because this is how many kneeling people the tomb can admit, and then they leave, to let other people, who keep waiting outside, take their turn. Overall, one has no time to delight in the All-Holy Pilgrimage sites, because there are so many people.

Nevertheless, even though the All-Holy Tomb closes at seven, you can remain inside the Resurrection Temple, if you obtain a special permission from the guards. Still, they don't let more than two to three people in. So, when the group of students and I visited the All-Holy Tomb, I went up to a guard and asked him, "Father, if some of the kids wish to remain in the temple during the evening, when it's closed, may we do it? Will you let us?" He answered, "You may. What is your number?" I told him, "Close to forty," and he asked again, "And how many of you wish to remain?" I had no clue, so I immediately asked the kids. "How many of you want to remain in the Temple of the Resurrection, in the All-Holy Tomb?" and everybody raised their hands! They all wanted to do it! So I returned to the guard of the All-Holy

Tomb, feeling sort of embarrassed, for I didn't know what to say! And when he asked me how many were those who wished to remain, I asked back, to make sure of the number allowed. He said, "Five to six persons." "Well, father, I guess it's kind of hard for me to choose, so it's rather difficult for us to remain." "Why? Don't you want to?" "Oh, yes, we do," I said, "but it's that everybody wants to. So, I don't know what we can do about it…" The guard was astonished. He stared at the kids, one after the other, and saw their faces portraying their quest for God, their thirst for Christ… A few minutes later, he told me: "Wait. I'll go ask permission from the Prior of the Resurrection Temple and I'll tell you what can be done." And he did, in fact, take permission, and he allowed, for the first time, so many people to remain inside the temple

As soon as I announced to the kids that we were allowed to stay, they were overwhelmed with joy and happiness. We returned in haste to the hotel, we ate a little something, in order to be able to hold out through the night, we took some water and warm clothes – for nights are cold – and we entered the Resurrection Temple.

I, too, felt infinite joy at being able to worship the All-Holy Tomb for quite a long time all by myself, because, during all previous visits, I was only able to remain in there from fifteen to thirty minutes. The feeling one experiences when touching the All-Holy Tomb is amazing. You place your hands, your lips, your cheeks, your forehead, you let your tears flow with emotion, you dedicate your whole being at that very moment. You can't draw away from Him. Hence, since we'd obtained permission to enter, I reckoned I would relish the visit, now that I had abundant time available to stay there. However, I didn't make it. Why? Because the kids wouldn't leave me alone, without first having me preach to them, asking me for advice and instructions; without having me explain to them how they would or should feel, to arouse in them a feeling of solemnity.

As a result, I remained in the All-Holy Tomb's antechamber, which is a piece of the rock the angel rolled away at the day of the Lord's Resurrection. I stood kneeling there, showing them how to enter in groups of two or three people and advising them to stay as long as they wished to. I thought to myself that they were young people, accustomed to the comforts of city life, so it was highly improbable they would remain inside the Tomb for more than a couple of minutes; after all, they would soon get bored – or that's what I imagined. Much to my surprise, though, they were not coming out! They were inside the All-Holy Tomb, touching the spot where Christ's body was laid down, and they were overcome by an intense thrill – the same thrill that had overwhelmed me too, even though I was still standing in the antechamber. The kids had felt the grace, and they could not turn away. And I saw, in the darkness, in the glow coming from the vigil lights, their eyes all wet with tears - tears of gratitude, joy, happiness, grandeur. They felt Christ, while Christ was not there, while His body was absent. Still, whereas the monument was empty, at the same time it was filled with the presence of our Lord, of our resurrected Lord, "in another form". The other Christ, now offered to us in another fashion. So, the kids stayed in there for a long time, almost twenty minutes each, and, although I wanted so much to enter, I didn't have the heart to do it. I saw how moved they were, some of them having a hard time coming out, and I felt deep inside that they could not get enough of this glory. Why? Because the Lord Is Risen. He is resurrected and He exists, and the kids felt this while they were in there, they grasped it.

What impressed me most, were the things they told me – wonderful, theological things. Bear in mind that they had never studied theology, for they were not students of theology – still, they knew how to theologize. When one touches Christ, he becomes a theologian. When one feels Christ's Resurrection, he is a theologian. So, one of the kids approached me and told me: "I understood something here. That Church is not an institution; it is not bureaucracy, nor a system, or a human creation. Church is a person. Church is Christ, Christ risen. I felt this... Inside the All-Holy Tomb, I felt the Lord." Another kid told me: "One wants to cry incessantly here, without knowing why. One wants to cry of happiness, of joy, of devoutness, of grandeur, of fulfilling and completeness of life. Touching the Lord makes one's eyes run with tears." So, this can't be a lie. There's no way a lie can make you feel this way. It was something real. Another student admitted: "Here, you feel that praying is the most natural thing in the world. It comes spontaneously. It's impossible not to pray in here, when you see Christ resurrected. You want to feel the Lord closer to you; you want to talk to Him, to confide in Him your problems, your anguishes, everything. You feel Him being alive, and once you feel that there is someone alive around you, by your side, you offer everything to Him. You maintain a live, personal relationship with Him." Another kid confessed to me: "My mind was occupied by thoughts. They tortured me for years; but from the day I went to worship the All-Holy Tomb of our Lord, where the Lord entered, only to come out resurrected and glorious, my mind was relieved and cleared from all those thoughts. I experienced a miracle. My life changed. I don't care if I saw the Holy Light or not. This is a light everyone can see. This is not what one should ask for himself. I was overjoyed, because I felt the Lord identical to a light within my heart." Could this be a fairy tale? Can this happen in an empty tomb? Do you know any other tomb offering hope and life like this?

There was this man, who used to say in his prayer: "My Tomb, my buttress, my rock, my consolation." This Tomb, this slab, is indeed our rock and our shield. The Salutations to the All-Holy Tomb address the All-Holy Tomb with wonderful apostrophes, qualifying it as Christ's bed. "Rejoice, end of Christ's passions…". That's where the Lord rested, in the All-Holy Tomb. That's where he rose from, and this shield, the slab of the All-Holy Tomb, makes the devil's arrows bend and break and melt away and vanish.

This time of year, I would suggest you read the Pentecostarion, the Holy Service book comprising of the hymns sung during the chanting Services, from Easter Sunday through to Pentecost, as I find it highly appropriate. I would also suggest another booklet produced by the Holy Monastery of the Paraclete, containing very deep meanings, especially for people who like poetic texts which are together philosophical, spiritual and theological. It is called "Word to the Blessed and God-receiving Tomb" and it is written by priest-monk Ioustinos. I believe it will really speak to you.

So, the Lord is risen. He is resurrected, worshipped, believed, sensed, but without any tangible evidence. I cannot draw an equation on a blackboard to prove that the Lord is risen, but, if I could take a look inside your heart, I am certain I would see the mark of His touch on it.

At the Via Dolorosa, Jerusalem, there is a spot, where the Lord is said to have fallen and to have leaned his hand against, leaving a mark. I don't know if the mark exists, but I know that the mark of Christ risen is in your heart, and this is huge proof for me. Everybody speaks of Christ. He is not absent. If He was absent, how come everybody speaks of Him? If He was absent, how come so many books are written on Him? Why do people comment on His life? Why do people fight Him? Who would waste his time on dead people? Who would comment on and bring to the forefront a person who died two thousand years ago? Nobody. Yet, everybody is occupied with the Lord, for He is alive, He exists and He moves among us. He exists within this world's history. He is interwoven in every event taking place, He rules our world. He governs history and He is discreetly hidden behind all human paths. He is our Lord. He is the Lord Who lives, substantiating the prophesy of Saint Symeon the God-Receiver to Mary, that "this child is set for the falling and the rising of many". Some will see Him and they will be tempted, they will trip and fall. They will not be able to accept Him by setting aside the rationalism with which they view life. Nevertheless, they will be people who will raise thanks to Him. Their soul will breathe; they will lift their eyes, they will let oxygen fill their hearts. "Behold, this child is set for the falling and the rising of many…, and for a sign which is spoken against… that the thoughts of many hearts may be revealed". That's the secret. Depending on the life you lead, you can see Christ or you cannot. Is your life clean? Or, do you want your life cleansed? Then you're not afraid of the light, you go towards Christ. You want to believe in Him and you ask Him for help, for the gift of faith. But there are those who don't want this, because "Everyone who does evil hates the light, and will not come into the light for fear that his deeds will be exposed." There are those who don't want their deeds revealed, for their deeds were performed in darkness and that's why they don't want Christ. They won't deal with Him. But there will come a time, when we shall see Him facing us – and then what will be our relation to Him, how will we have prepared ourselves for this meeting?

Just take a look at how many books are written for and against the Lord. How many movies, perspectives and theories exist on His person and how many trends were born about Him through the centuries? Everybody revolves around the Lord. No other person, no other founder of a religion has been as controversial as Jesus Christ. Everybody deals with Him. The whole of humanity, brethren, was represented on Golgotha. The thief on the right and the thief on the left, the grateful and the ungrateful thief. Humanity takes a stand. We are the ones to decide, whether we will take side and stand by the grateful thief, repeating his words: "Lord, we accept Thee; Lord, remember me when Thou comest into Thy Kingdom". He called Him Lord. "My Lord, my God, I accept You as Master of the world, as Master of the universe, I accept that You exist and that You are True God." "How can I remember you, my poor thief, my poor child?" asked the Lord. "How can I remember you, since I'll be dead in a short while, since we'll both pass away? How can you ask of me to remember you? Into my Kingdom... What is this Kingdom? Does this mean that you accept me as King? You accept that I'm alive? You accept that in a little while, when I will have drawn my last breath, I will continue to live and that I will be King in a Kingdom resplendent with light?" "Yes! Yes!" the thief answered. "I accept that You're alive!" So, there it is. Some people accept that the Lord is alive, even though they see Him during His Passion, "speckled with bruises and all-mighty in operation". Covered with marks of wounds, sore, and Almighty. "All-mighty in operation," for He has strength and power. "I believe in You, Lord. I believe that, while You're dying, You are alive. You are alive, true conqueror of death. Conqueror of decay. You conquer everything. That's why I believe in

You." This one's our thief. You are standing behind this thief, right now, for you listen, you believe and you worship the Lord's Resurrection. The rest of humanity, the other part, is standing next to the ungrateful thief, the one who challenges Christ, the one who asks for yet another miracle and does not realize that he is already facing a miracle, the miracle of the Lord crucified. And he asks of the Lord to get down of the Cross, in order to be seen saving Himself and saving them too. In other words, he puts God to the test; he plays around with Him, as much as with his own salvation. And, in the end, he loses salvation. So, there it is, the whole of humanity on Golgotha. But we want to stand alongside the grateful thief and to declare: "Lord, we want to believe that You are alive, risen, a living reality by our side..." This is what the Lord is, someone Who exists close to us.

It is, therefore, awesome believing in the Lord's Resurrection. It is an experience so strong, that it leaves one afraid of nothing: lifelong adventures, shipwrecks, persecutions, whippings, martyrdom, ultimately death, after the example of Apostle Paul, of all the Holy Apostles, of all the Holy Martyrs. All the Holy Apostles died for the Lord, they martyred for Him. I believe that only one or two of them left this world in a peaceful manner. They all were martyred for the Lord, suffering terrible pains, yet believing that it was worth it, since Christ is risen, His resurrection being a fact they saw and felt within their hearts.

You can't lie, brother, and change the whole world. The world doesn't change with fairy tales. All those exquisite temples cannot be built; superb civilizations, such as the Byzantine one, cannot emerge, based on a lie. All those things accomplished thanks to Christianity's influence in the world cannot be based on a lie. A lie does not hold such a transformational power. A lie does not pacify man; it does not appease his soul. A lie brings about disturbance, void, lack of satisfaction. There are people, belonging to the Church, who get delirious from Christ's love and from the sense of His Resurrection. They rush into the streets crying, "Lord, we can't contain all this joy we feel being close to You! We cannot contain anymore all this happiness You're granting us..." A lie cannot make you say such things. I've never seen anybody going to a concert, a political rally, anyplace at all, and then returning home and trying to convince everybody, "Be like me. I've discovered the secret of happiness. This is what true joy is about - what I believe in." Nobody does this. All they come down to is return home tired, worn out, psychologically, physically and existentially spent, and going to bed depressed and melancholic. On the other hand, when you go to church, you feel joyous. Other people look at you and see that what you feel is true. I once asked someone who had just come out of church, "How are you? Are you happy?" – and he answered, "Doesn't it show?" He sensed that the joy he experienced by being close to Christ radiates and shows outwardly.

During these days, I suggest that you read the Acts of the Apostles, because these texts reflect exactly what Resurrection implies in the practice of life. The Acts of the Apostles are precisely the action of the Holy Spirit, the acts of Christ risen through the hands and the existence of the Holy Apostles. That's where you'll find out what Christ risen accomplished through His use of the Holy Apostles, the miracles our Lord performed, the changing of the world, the transformation of their souls. And this is proof enough that the Resurrection is dynamic. It is something that transforms and changes man. The Lord is alive and resurrected.

You should not feel envious of 30 C.E. Jerusalem, nor of the Holy Land of the era, wishing you'd been living then and there. Listen to what Saint Chrysostom says. You are better off now. Right now, you believe in Christ and your faith in His Resurrection is a powerful experience, much more powerful than if you were living back then. If you were living in that era, you might not believe in Christ in the way you believe now – with the Holy Spirit, with the Holy Sacraments, after twenty centuries of Christianity, in the course of which you have evidence of so many miracles, of a long parade of saints. Of those who lived to see Him back then, some called Him misled, possessed, and liar. They wanted to deny Him. They didn't believe Him. They saw Him, yet they could not comprehend Him. You don't see Him, and yet you believe in Him. You have not touched Him, like Apostle Thomas, yet you say, "My Lord and God." You live in a different era, but you have the Lord within you, by sacramentally coming into communion with Him, by receiving His Body and His Blood – and this is something people of that era did not experience. They might have seen Him with their physical eyes, but they didn't touch Him with their soul's eyes. We have an advantage over them, as Saint John Chrysostom says, for they saw a simple man. But we understand that He is our Saviour, our Lord, the Almighty, Most-Merciful God, and we feel infinite wonderment, because we have seen the Lord's course through our twenty-century human history, we have seen what Christ means.

It was not the Lord who let down humanity during these twenty centuries. It was us, who disappointed Him and who abandoned Him. He is faithful to His promises. And the fact that the world is going haywire, despite the Lord's Resurrection, is due to our not adopting the gifts of the Resurrection as our own. He showered us with gifts, but we did not reach out to take them and make them our own. He offers us the water of immortality, and we willingly seal our mouths, not wanting to drink from this water. It is not Christ's fault that our lives do not rise. It's our fault, for keeping ourselves under lock and key, inside the shell of our egotism, and for not opening our hearts in order for them to receive Christ. We do not worship the Lord, neither we, or our politicians, or the masters of this world. They do not worship Christ, and this is the reason why they don't let all the good of the resurrection flow into our homeland and into the whole world. The Lord would have given us everything, if only we accomplished what the prayer of the Resurrection says, "Having seen the Resurrection of Christ, let us worship Holy Lord Jesus." "Having seen." We saw the Resurrection. We saw a specific event, a specific moment in time. We saw the Lord's Resurrection and, since we saw it, we worship Him. "Let us worship." Let us worship Lord Jesus. But, who does this? Do you worship the Lord, or do you worship your ego? Does your life change? The Lord is risen; He pours His gifts unto us, He brings forgiveness, absolution, mercy, reconciliation with God. He reminds us that we are His beloved children, that Heaven is waiting for us. Yes! All these are offered for those who wish to receive them. Christ Is Risen. Still, are you risen? Are you changed? Did anything die within you in order for something new to be born? Did you change His victory into your own victory? Did you change His glory into your own glory? Have you received the Lord risen within you? Christ Is Risen. Are you still afraid of death? Do you still feel desperation, melancholy, fear and panic when faced with the perishable nature of your existence? If you're still afraid, it means you haven't grasped the meaning of the Lord's Resurrection.

"Having seen the Resurrection of Christ." This is no fairy tale. This is a reality. When the Saints wrote these resurrectional prayers, they weren't writing just well-turned, bogus words. These words were the essence of their hearts and the overflow of their souls. Yet we, today, exclaim these very words for the eyes of the world. It seems as though we're in a museum and we just read the books included in its collections – words that some people wrote a long time ago. But what they wrote back then, they experienced it. We just parrot the words, missing their essence, letting it slip through our fingers. Their words were fiery. They came from their hearts which really experienced them, and this is the reason they wrote them, because they felt the need to do it and to keep alive their souls' experience.

When I was at the Holy Mountain Athos, four years ago, there was a really blessed and holy monk named Father Ioannikios – I am mentioning this, because he is no longer alive - at the monastery of Dionysios. After Easter, during the Easter week, I approached him and I asked him, "Father, Lent has passed; tell me something. What did you feel during this year's Lent, this Easter? Offer a message for me. What touched your soul? What did the Lord send you as a gift?" And, do you know what he answered, humbly, very down-to-earth and very truthfully? "You know," he said, "what I understood? That a whole God dies and is risen, and I don't understand anything." That's what he told me. "I remain unchanged and therefore I understand how cold-hearted, insensitive and ungrateful I am." He was a holy man, though, who passed away due to a painful illness. On his face you could see the patience, the sweet joy that the Resurrection inspired in him, the courage, the hope; and he did not utter a single moan while he was lying in pain on his bed, for he was truly humbled, as his words demonstrated. That man felt the Resurrection, he decoded it into his everyday life and on his dying bed. He withstood death, pain, the illness that consumed him, because he had indeed touched Christ risen.

All these are not fairy tales, brethren. I cannot prove them by logical means, but I am certain, deep inside, for what I'm telling you right now. Yet, if some of you believe that it might be a fairy tale – well, for me, it is the most beautiful fairy tale in the whole world, and I experience it as my truth. Besides, everybody in our days is living a mere myth, a lie. Wherever you turn your eyes, you see posters and ads exhorting you to live your myth, your lie! They prompt you to depend on something, so that you will be able to survive. So, even if there are people who prefer to call all this a fairy tale, then I have to tell you that it is the most powerful one and that it contains amazing truths. It contains the truth of life and death.

If what I believe is a fairy tale, then how could we explain that I am able to live, to withstand pain, to face death and smile, to go to the cemetery and plant flowers - and then, when I see pain coming my way, I am able to have patience? Even if an earthquake hit me, I would stand erect just the same. Whatever might come my way – a shipwreck, frustration, bitterness, sickness, betrayal, loneliness, sorrow – I can withstand everything. Who helps me withstand? Who makes me live? You're saying that what you're experiencing is true, at least more true than my own version. I accept this. Can your truth keep you standing strong like this? You claim that I believe in a fairy tale. Ok, then, show me - what do you have to follow, what is it that backs you up? What will save you from the menace of death, of nullification, of the decay and panic involved in termination? For you know very well that whatever we get down to shall eventually come to an end. How will you be able to bear this? Death comes. How will you conquer it? My lie is truer – and it is so, because it is merely the truth, a truth that can't be factually proved, but only from the depths of your heart. Father Paisios used a particular verb to express this truth. He said that it is something that must be lived, that it must be experienced.

Brethren, I wish that all of us, through every life's adventure, through every blow and every pain, shall finally comprehend the Lord's Resurrection and shall turn to Him for strength, that we shall turn to this empty monument, so that we'll be able to withstand every pain in life, every sorrow, and to say from within our hearts that "Christ Is Risen."

FR ANDREAS KONANOS

Father Andreas Konanos was born in Munich in 1970. He comes from Ioannina, lived in Munich and from 1977 in Athens. He finished high school in the classical High School and studied Theology in Athens. Blessed Archbishop Christodoulos ordained him deacon in 1999 and Elder Archimandrite in 2000. He took over the parish of student meetings, vigils, speeches and lectures at parents' schools and spiritual centres of the Archdiocese of Athens. In 2006 he began the broadcast "Unseen Crossings" at the Radio Station Church of Piraeus. This broadcast led to invitations to speak in many cities in Greece, Cyprus and America. His contact with Jerusalem, Mount Athos and Elders inside and outside Mount Athos are a source of strength in his life.